NOBODY'S PERFECT

NOBODY'S PERFECT

TWO MEN, ONE CALL, AND A GAME FOR BASEBALL HISTORY

ARMANDO GALARRAGA
JIM JOYCE
WITH **DANIEL PAISNER**

Atlantic Monthly Press
New York

Published simultaneously in Canada
Printed in the United States of America

FIRST EDITION

ISBN-13: 978-0-8021-1988-9

Atlantic Monthly Press
an imprint of Grove/Atlantic, Inc.
841 Broadway
New York, NY 10003

Distributed by Publishers Group West

www.groveatlantic.com

11 12 13 14   10 9 8 7 6 5 4 3 2 1

My part of this book is written especially for my family. They are
the ones who believe in me, no matter what.

A.G.

To Kay, Jimmy, and Keri, for their undying
LOVE and SUPPORT.
To Ellouise and Jim Joyce, my mom and dad . . . I miss you, Dad!
To Tim, Amy, Christopher, Julia, and Jessica.
To Armando Galarraga, who is the real story here.
To Marty Springstead, for making me the umpire I am today.
To the umpires of Major League Baseball, for their support.
To Nick, for your inspiration and perspective . . . *spilt milk?*

JJ.

To my children—Jake, Hana, and Rose. May the examples
of these good men stand as a reminder that,
sometimes, humanity happens.

D.P.

From the benches, black with people, there went up a muffled roar,
Like the beating of the storm-waves on a stern and distant shore.
"Kill him! Kill the umpire!" shouted someone on the stand;
And it's likely they'd a-killed him had not Casey raised his hand.

—Ernest Thayer, "Casey at the Bat"

Contents

SETUP

On June 2, 2010, Detroit Tigers pitcher Armando Galarraga retired the first twenty-six batters he faced in a game against the Cleveland Indians at Comerica Park in Detroit. The twenty-eight-year-old Venezuelan was making only his fourth appearance of the season and hoping to reestablish himself in the Tigers rotation after starting the year with the Toledo Mud Hens, the Tigers' Triple-A affiliate, so it felt to him like he needed to make an especially strong showing.

And he was doing just that.

By the middle innings, even a casual fan could sense it was a magical, memorable night. Whatever Galarraga had been out to prove, he had already made his point. And now, as the ninth inning unfolded, he was poised to become just the twenty-first pitcher in the history of Major League Baseball to record a perfect game—a once-a-generation achievement that had somehow been accomplished twice in the previous month. The young pitcher had thrown a mere eighty pitches—only eighteen of them out of the strike zone. His command was pitch-perfect; his confidence, off the charts.

If Galarraga had set out to show the Detroit Tigers that he could be a dominant pitcher, he had certainly succeeded, and now he was one out away from owning a special place in baseball history and securing his spot with the big club for the foreseeable future.

And then, Galarraga's pitch for baseball immortality turned in an instant. Cleveland infielder Jason Donald hit a sharp grounder to the right side of the diamond. Detroit first baseman

Miguel Cabrera fielded the ball cleanly and made a neat, soft toss to Galarraga, who had swiftly crossed to cover first. It seemed to the pitcher like he had beaten a hustling Jason Donald to the first-base bag, but first-base umpire Jim Joyce believed otherwise. He called the batter safe, setting in motion an angry swirl of second-guessing and hair pulling among the Detroit crowd.

In Joyce's mind, just then, it wasn't even close.

Tiger manager Jim Leyland came out to argue the call. Tiger players screamed at Joyce from the dugout, from the field, from the bullpen. Only Galarraga appeared to take the call in stride, and he returned to the mound with a smile on his face that seemed incongruous with the bitter disappointment that filled the stadium. He said later that he was feeling too happy to feel too sad. But suddenly it was difficult for the young pitcher to focus. The ball no longer felt familiar in his grip, and the idea that he could go back to his game plan and make good things happen was now just out of reach. Still, he managed to coax Cleveland lead-off hitter Trevor Crowe to ground out to third baseman Brandon Inge to end the game, giving the pitcher a one-hit shutout and a cone of spotlight he couldn't think how to fill.

At the same time, veteran umpire Jim Joyce was thrust into a spotlight all his own. A dedicated and respected professional determined to leave his own mark on the game by getting it right each time out, Joyce had a sick feeling as he left the field that he might have just botched the most important call of his career. He ran the play over and over in his mind and worried he might have missed something. It gnawed at him, this worry, left him thinking he had just gotten in the way of history. He went from thinking the play wasn't even close in one direction, to thinking it wasn't even close in the other. He reviewed the play on tape and addressed the media immediately following the game, tearfully admitting he had missed the call and apologizing to Galarraga for erasing his bid for baseball immortality. "This is a history call," Joyce told reporters after the game, "and I kicked the shit out of it."

Over in the players locker room, Galarraga shrugged off Joyce's call, saying, "Nobody's perfect." He smiled as he said this, and he continued to smile as he met with reporters in the next hours, days, weeks. It never occurred to Galarraga to blame the umpire for costing him a perfect game. He was having too much fun, the young pitcher remarked in the game's drawn-out aftermath, to let a small disappointment dampen his fine performance.

It wasn't about forgiveness, he said, because there was nothing to forgive. It was just one of the breaks of the game. Galarraga was merely grateful for the opportunity to shine on such an important stage, to show his teammates what he could do, and to make an argument for a long major league career. "This was my best game so far," he said at one point, and he could only look ahead to more of the same, not back to what he could not change.

Meanwhile, the rest of the world took note. Joyce's call was debated and dissected in newspapers all over the country—and played and replayed on television and on the Internet. It was featured on the front page of the New York Times *and on all three network newscasts. Sports-radio talk shows lit up with callers weighing in on what was right about the game of baseball, and what was wrong, and whether or not Joyce's call should be allowed to stand. Baseball writers, team executives, and league officials discussed the merits of allowing video review technology to assist umpires with close calls. Michigan governor Jennifer*

Granholm issued a proclamation declaring that Galarraga had indeed pitched a perfect game—at least in the eyes of the state of Michigan. The White House press secretary joked that he would prepare an executive order to get Major League Baseball commissioner Bud Selig to overturn Joyce's call and award the pitcher a perfect game after the fact. Joyce received death threats from angry fans, while Galarraga received proposals of marriage from young women (and their fathers!) charmed by the way he carried himself in the ensuing storm.

It was, for a sweet, enduring moment, a play that transcended the game itself.

PROLOGUE

ARMANDO GALARRAGA

My Blessings

Here is the first thing I think when I see the umpire make the safe sign at first base: I think he is kidding. I think the only reason he can say the runner is safe is to make a joke, because it does not feel to me like the play is even close.

Why do I say this? Because I have been playing baseball since I was a small boy. I know how the umpire can say one thing and you cannot complain because you cannot be certain. But I do not think this is one of those times, because it cannot be so. I know with my own eyes what I have just seen. And it is not only with my eyes. I know by listening. I know when my foot touches the base. I know when the batter touches the base.

I can feel these things, because I am a part of them. They do not happen one on top of the other, which is how it feels when you make a close play, both things at the same time. No, they happen one after the other. First there is my foot on the base, and then there is Jason Donald, the Cleveland batter, there is his foot on the base, and then there is the umpire Jim Joyce saying he is safe. It all happens in a row, one thing after the other, but the third thing is not connected to the first two, which is why I now think it must be a joke. Or a mistake. Or maybe my mind is playing tricks, because it cannot be that the umpire really means the batter is safe.

It cannot be that I will not have a perfect game after all. I cannot think such a thing. There are two outs in the ninth inning, and my friend Miguel Cabrera makes a nice play on a ground ball to the right side and I run to first and catch the ball and step on the base in time to beat the runner, like we practice all the time in spring training, over and over, and now the umpire is saying this is not how it happened.

I wonder why he is saying this. There is not a lot of time for thinking, but this is what I think. I wonder what he has seen that I have not seen, what he has felt that I have not felt. I wonder what he has heard. I do not know Jim Joyce, except by his voice. The other players say he is a good umpire. They say he is fair, and I do not know any different. I will tell you the truth: I do not always pay attention to who is umpiring on the bases. When they are the home plate umpire, I pay only a little attention. I do not know them by name, only by how they call balls and strikes, so that is how I know Jim Joyce, by his voice. Other pitchers, they study the umpires and know about their strike zones, but I believe there are other things to worry about. I have my plan, going into a game. And the home plate umpire, he has his plan. He does not have to know about my plan and I do not have to know about his plan and we can both do our jobs. So all I know about Jim Joyce is that when he is the umpire behind home plate his calls are loud. He makes sure everybody knows what he thinks. It is like he is making an announcement after every pitch. This is what everybody says, the other pitchers on my team. And it is the same at first base, each time he calls a runner safe or out. You can hear him in every part of the stadium.

So it is not possible that I have not heard the umpire properly, when he shouts that the runner is safe. There is no room for misunderstanding, and as soon as I hear his call I turn and see him standing behind the base, with his arms wide, making the safe sign, so there is no misunderstanding this as well. This is no joke. This is not my brain playing tricks.

The second thing I think is that it does not matter. Okay, so it is not the call I am expecting, but I am too happy, so it does not matter. I am too happy with how I am pitching and how I have reached all the way to the end of the game without allowing one of the Cleveland Indians batters to get on base. It is such a joyful moment that nothing can make me sad. It is a perfect, perfect game, and I realize that nothing can change the truth of this perfect, perfect game. I tell this to people later and they do not believe me, but this is how I feel. Suddenly, I realize this. I know in my heart that I have now completed my perfect game. The moment my foot touches first base, I know this. It is something to share with my father. It is something to tell to my children and my grandchildren. It is something the people of Venezuela will always remember. And so I do not think to complain, because I was taught not to complain. The umpire is in charge. If he says the runner is safe, then the runner is safe. That is all.

The only thing for me to do is feel proud of the work I have already done, and worry about the next batter, and remember my many blessings. I do not do such a good job of this, worrying about the next batter, because I no longer have my focus. I am not upset but I am now thinking of other things besides baseball. I am thinking that I have so many blessings, so many reasons to smile. I am too happy, so I cannot be too sad when Jim Joyce calls the runner safe at first base. The fans are cheering for me. My teammates on the Detroit Tigers are cheering for me. It is a nice night, early in the season, and we are playing good baseball, so why should I not be happy? I am being paid to play baseball, a game I love, so why should I not be smiling? I have just pitched the best game of my career. And now there is a runner on first base and I am still pitching the best game of my career.

I am thinking, *Armando, if you keep pitching like this there will be many more chances for a perfect game.*

I am thinking, *Sometimes the umpire knows one thing and you know another and there is nothing to do about this.*

I am thinking, *Let us just worry about the next batter, and then we can celebrate the blessings of this game.*

I do not yell or curse or kick at the dirt, because what do I have to yell or curse or kick about? I can disagree. I can question. But I cannot argue because I cannot complain. I am filled with so many blessings, so here is what I do: I smile. I have not done anything wrong. Instead, I have done everything right. For the whole game, I do not think I have thrown a bad pitch. The ball can only do what I want it to do, what I tell it to do. I cannot remember a time when I have been pitching so well, for so long. For a batter or two, yes, I can feel like I am in control, I can feel like I am dominating. For an inning or two, maybe I can feel these things, I can feel like the best pitcher in the history of baseball. But never for a whole game. Never before this one night.

So, of course, I smile.

JIM JOYCE

Tossing, Turning

Can't sleep.

It's three-thirty in the morning and I'm sitting in the front room of my mother's house, chain-smoking Winston Lights. Same house I grew up in. Same chair where my father used to sit. Same shadows on the wall from where the streetlights come in through the picture window.

The house is finally quiet, but there are noises in my head. Calls I should have made. Shouts I never thought I'd hear from players, fans, grounds crew guys. Can't shut them out for trying. I've got the front door open, to get a breeze going. It's a warm night, the a/c is off, but I'm mostly hoping the night sounds will drown out my thoughts, help me relax.

Yeah, right.

Some sounds take you from your troubles, and others remind you of them. Tonight, there's just a bunch of reminders. Like my cell phone: I'd put the thing on vibrate, but after one or two in the morning, when there's no whoosh of cars going up and down our street, even a vibrating cell phone can make a lot of noise, so I switch it to silent. It's still lighting up every couple minutes, but at least I don't have to listen to it. Just have to watch it keep lighting the room with how I messed up.

My eighty-six-year-old mother went to bed a couple hours ago. She waited up for me—dozing in her chair by the television. I came in just before the eleven o'clock news. My timing couldn't have been better. Or worse. The phone rang as I walked in the front door. For all I know, it had been ringing and ringing, so here it was, ringing again . . . or still. One of those. Either way, it was late to be calling my mother's house.

I said, "Don't answer it."

My mother looked up from her dozing. She said, "Why not?"

I said, "I'm not very popular right now, that's why."

She said, "What happened, Jimmy? How was the game?"

I fell into my dad's chair, across the couch from my mom. I said, "You didn't watch?" If she had watched, she wouldn't have been asking.

She said, "No, I was watching something else. First the game, then something else. Then I fell asleep."

This was unusual for my mother. She always watches my games. She always asks, and I tell her the time and channel. But I didn't worry about this, just then. Instead, I explained. I said, "I kicked a call. Last play of the game. Cost a kid a chance at history." I told her what it meant to pitch a perfect game—no hits, no walks, no errors, no blemishes of any kind—and she nodded like she understood. Wasn't so long ago she would have known this for herself. Been watching baseball since she met my father, but now her memory is off and on and she had to be reminded.

She said, "It's not such a big thing, Jimmy. It's only a game."

I said, "Yeah, but I don't know how it happened. The whole game, nobody made a mistake but me."

She said, "I don't know why anyone would be mad at you, Jimmy. You did your best. You always do your best."

I said, "Oh, Mom, come on."

Just then the local news came on. Like it was waiting for me. Like it had something to tell me I didn't already know. I'd kicked that call, and now it was the top story. Nothing was more important, in the eyes of these television news people. The economy was in the toilet. People all around Detroit were out of work, scrambling while the big three automakers figured how to fix their business. There was a war going on in Iraq, another in Afghanistan, and an out-of-control oil spill in the Gulf of Mexico killing the coastline. But this one baseball game, with this kid pitcher coming this close to a perfect game, this was the big headline.

The drill, when I work a game in Detroit, is I stay at my mom's house in Toledo. Only takes about forty-five minutes to get to the stadium, so it's a good chance to visit. Same goes for Cleveland—also not such a bad drive. Been doing it since I started calling games in the bigs. It's become a soft spot in a tough schedule, something to look forward to on the long slog of a season. Usually, two or three times a year, I'll come through one or the other, make a true homestand out of it, only this season is the first without my dad. He died almost exactly a year ago, so there's some bittersweet to it, me coming home like this. Just yesterday, I took my mom out to the cemetery. First chance I had to see my dad's headstone, first time I'd been to his grave since the funeral. Still can't get over that he's gone—especially now, this time of year.

He was the one who got me into baseball. Guess you could say he was the one who got me into umpiring, only not really. Back when I was still playing—high school, first couple years of college—he started working youth and amateur games all around the state. Pee Wee, Colt, Junior Knothole . . . all the way through to the high school circuit. Don't think he liked it too much. Don't think he liked the way folks would go after him when they didn't like a call. Wasn't really his thing, in the end, but he made a good go of it. Worked at it a couple years before moving on to something else. Still, first thing I thought of, soon as I realized I'd kicked the call, was him not being here. One of those fleeting, racing thoughts that just rip through your head. I thought, *It's a good thing he's not here to see this.* I thought, *A call like this, it'd just about kill him.*

Said as much to my wife Kay when she called after the game to see how I was doing. Said, "He would have just died."

She said, "Stop it, Jim. Don't do this to yourself."

I half listened as the news anchor said I'd made one of the worst calls in baseball history, called the runner safe when he was clearly out. They showed the replay but I couldn't watch. Once was about all I could take, back in the umpires locker room right after the game: yeah, okay, the runner was clearly out. No reason to have to look at it again. When I made the call, in my head the runner beat the ball. Wasn't even close.

But then when I played it back, in my gut the ball got there first. Wasn't even close. And now I had to fit those two pieces together in a way that made sense.

When other guys mess up on the job, they hang their heads and hope like crazy their boss doesn't notice. Me, I mess up and it's this huge deal—so, absolutely, I couldn't sleep. Tried, for a bit. Stayed up talking to my mom for a while, about this and that. Anything but the game. Spoke to Kay back home in Oregon. She'd called when I was driving out from the stadium, and another few times to make sure I was okay. Told me to delete my Facebook account.

Hadn't even thought of that. I said, "Is it that bad?"

She said, "Don't worry about it, Jim. Just don't look at it."

At a time like this, you trust your wife to tell you what to do. She would have canceled the account herself if she knew my password. She only wished she could have gotten the same message to the kids, she said. Already, just a couple hours after the game, they'd each gotten about fifty ugly, threatening messages, and it tore me up to hear this because, of course, those messages were meant for me.

When my mom finally went to bed, I went to the kitchen and grabbed a can of Diet Coke from the fridge, figured I'd sit and sip and smoke. And think. But then when my thinking didn't take me anywhere I wanted to go, I went up to my old bedroom and changed into a T-shirt and shorts. One thing: my room is set up like it was when I was a kid. Sun comes in through the shades first thing in the morning, same way I remember. Bed, dresser . . . everything in the same place. Different furniture, after all these years, but set up the same way. It's not a museum or anything, doesn't look like Richie Cunningham's room from the 1950s, but some nights I fall down dead tired after a tough game and it's like I'm back in high school. Like I never left. Only things my mom has kept the same are the bed frame and the picture of Jesus, Mary, and Joseph on the wall. Must've had that picture fifty, sixty years—and here it is, still watching over me.

I wondered where the hell they'd been, Jesus, Mary, and Joseph, just a couple hours earlier, when I could have used some watching over.

I killed the lights and sat on my bed for a bit. Then I lay down. I knew I wouldn't be able to sleep. Talked myself into it before even trying, but now I told myself I had to at least try, so I lay there a good long while, eyes closed, trying to drift off but at the same time knowing I wouldn't.

Hard not to beat myself up over something like this. Hard not to wish it away. There'd only been, what, twenty perfect games in major league history? Twenty, going back over one hundred and thirty years. It's probably the most difficult thing to do on a baseball diamond, keep the other team from getting on base, and here this big, sweet kid from Venezuela had done just that. Just about. Pitched a beautiful game. In complete control. Didn't waste a single pitch. Got to two outs in the ninth inning without allowing a base runner.

Twenty-six up, twenty-six down.

No hits, no runs, no errors.

And then the number nine hitter hits a hard grounder to the first baseman and I slide-step into position to make the call. I have a perfect angle on the play. It happens right in front of me. I see the runner bust it down the line, the pitcher bust it across the diamond to cover the bag . . . and I make the wrong call. Can't explain it. Can't understand it. I just missed it, is all. I saw it one way and the rest of the world saw it another.

Must've been twenty, thirty minutes I lay there like that, visualizing the play, putting myself back on that field. After a while I went back to my dad's old chair in the front room, where the can of Diet Coke was still waiting for me. Cigarettes, too. And that's where I am now, rooted to the very spot where my dad used to do his sitting and thinking, and I'm running the play over and over in my mind. It's all I can think about.

At some point I start to think about tomorrow, which of course is already today. Day game back in Detroit and I've got the plate. That's always a big deal, when you're calling balls and strikes. I need to be sharp. Today especially. Folks will be looking at me, hard. Riding me, hard. Can't afford to be off my game. Can't ever afford to be off my game, but this game especially. I work the clock in my head, figure I'll have to leave the house by eleven, eleven-fifteen, to be in the locker room my usual hour and a half before the game. Then I look at the clock and see that it's already five o'clock in the morning, so now the idea of sleep has a little more urgency to it. I don't want to be horseshit for the game. I know I'll have to face some heat when I get to the stadium, so I shuffle back to bed.

I hit the pillow and I'm gone.

Next thing I notice it's five-thirty and I'm all the way awake, and I tell myself again there's no way I'm catching any more sleep. Doesn't even feel to me like the sleep I managed to grab has done me any good, so I haul myself out of bed and into the kitchen. Make a pot of coffee. Sit myself down at the dinette table. Same spot I used to sit at when I was a kid. Fire up my first cigarette of the day, even though it really isn't. Get back to sitting, smoking, thinking, wondering how I can possibly work the plate this afternoon on so little sleep—and how I can possibly not.

ONE

Caracas

When you grow up playing baseball you never think you will pitch a perfect game. You dream about it, but you never think it will happen. It is such an impossible dream. A part of you might think, *Yes, this is something that can happen for me,* but there is a much bigger part that will be thinking, *No, it is not possible.* It is something to think about for motivation, but it cannot be something to think about for real because it is more than real. It is something for history, a goal most players can never reach, but a part of you believes it is a goal you can always reach whenever you start a new game.

This is one of the beautiful things about baseball. Every game is fresh and new. Anything is possible, even a perfect game. If you can get one out as a pitcher then you can get two, and then if you can get two you can get three, all the way through the lineup, all the way to a perfect game. It is in reach and out of reach. It is yes and no. It is possible and not possible. It is all these things, all at once.

I did not always think I would be a pitcher, so in the beginning I was not thinking about perfect games at all. When I was little, I played shortstop and centerfield, so for me the dream was to hit a home run to win a game or to make a great play in the field. I practiced making diving catches, and how I would watch the ball go over the fence if I ever hit a home run. I was not the best player, I was not the best hitter, but I was okay. I was somewhere in the middle. I was a good athlete, but nobody ever told me I could be a professional baseball player. I was tall and skinny and superhyper.

This is what my parents always said about me, that I was so active. I was always busy, busy, busy. Everything about my life was very fast, always moving, and as a boy this was mostly about sports. I did not only play baseball. I also played soccer. My father played soccer at the university, so we were always playing. Even today, my father is playing soccer, and when I was little my friends liked to play soccer, much more than baseball. I do not know why this was so, because all around Venezuela small boys were playing baseball. It was only with my friends that soccer was so important. For baseball, a few of us would play in a league, but soccer was for every day. Soccer was for whenever we wanted, however we wanted. We walked up and down the streets with our soccer ball, looking for games. We would say, "Let's go kick, let's go play." Three-on-three, five-on-five, whatever we could find. We would play until the sun fell from the sky, and even then sometimes we would keep playing.

Baseball was more organized, more formal. We played in a league, not like soccer. There were parents and coaches and umpires, so we could not always be ourselves. There were rules. There was keeping score. We could not just be a group of boys playing. I do not say this to complain or criticize but only to say how it was, only to make a comparison. Sometimes I wonder how I became a baseball player instead of a soccer player because soccer was more joyful. It was more natural. Do not misunderstand, I loved playing baseball, but when I was with my friends kicking the ball we were relaxed, like boys. I loved this, too, only in a different way.

In America, people say baseball is the national game. In Venezuela, this is true as well, even though we played so much soccer. Everybody in Venezuela knows about baseball and takes special pride in Venezuelan players who have played in the United States, in the major leagues. They are like national heroes, these players. We have our own players, our own teams, our own professional league: *Liga Venezolana de Béisbol Profesional*. In Caracas, the big team is *Leones del Caracas*, the Caracas Lions. This was the team I always cheered for. They are like the Yankees of Venezuela. They are always winning. We looked up to the *Leones* players and copied their batting styles or their pitching motions, trying to be like them so we could get noticed and play professional baseball, too.

From the small village where I was born, Cumana, there have been many players to make it to the major leagues, but they are not very famous outside Venezuela. From Caracas, where we moved when I was still a small boy, there have been a great many more, and some of them are very famous all over the world. One of the most famous is Andrés Galarraga, and I heard many things about him when I was growing up because we had the same family name. We are not related but I felt a special connection to him, even though I also felt a special connection to all of the players who were born in Caracas. Henry Blanco, Freddy Garcia, Magglio Ordonez, Omar Vizquel . . . so many great players, almost too many to mention.

I cheered for other players, too. Ken Griffey Jr. was probably my very favorite. I would stand in front of a mirror for many hours, trying to make my swing look like his swing. I tried to throw like him, run like him, catch like him . . . I wanted to do everything with the grace of Ken Griffey Jr. We all copied him. You could watch one of our games and almost every player would stand like Griffey in the batter's box, straight and tall, flapping his arms while he waited for the pitch.

It is a funny thing that Ken Griffey Jr. was my favorite player when I was little, because the day of my perfect, perfect game—June 2, 2010—was also the day he retired. It is like our two careers are connected to each other, like I am coming when he is going. The year before, I pitched my best game of the season against Seattle. I allowed only one hit and one run in seven innings. I pitched to Griffey three times and each time I was able to get him out: fly ball, pop fly, line drive. Two times, he hit the ball hard, but it did not matter. It would not have even mattered if he got a base hit, or a home run, because he was the great Ken Griffey Jr. Usually, when I am pitching, I am very good at concentrating, but that time I was not so good. I looked at Griffey making the same motions with his bat that I used to make when I was a small boy and I kept thinking, *Hey, I am pitching to Ken Griffey Jr.!*

I do not think I would have minded so much if I gave him a home run.

Some of my earliest memories playing baseball were with my father. His name is Jose, but everybody calls him Pepe. He worked as a manager in a big factory that made croissants. How he got this job, I never really understood, because at the university he studied marine biology. He worked with microscopes. For a time he could only find work as a teacher, but he did not want to be a teacher, so as a young man he took this job in the croissant factory. I do not think he even knew about croissants, but it was a respectable job, so this was what he did. The money was good and he had an important place in the company. I always liked this job because my father brought home fresh croissants, and also because he had time for me and sports. He believed very much in sports and physical activity. He believed it was a good and valuable thing for a boy in Caracas to play sports. If you were running around playing sports, your body would be healthy and you would not have time to get into trouble. You would be forced to make good, positive choices.

I have an older sister, Bethzalie, and we all called her Bethza. She was not very athletic, but my father made a special effort with me and sports. With my sister, he encouraged her to do other things. With me, the encouragement was for sports. He bought me my first glove, a Tamanaco glove. In Venezuela, Tamanaco is a big company for sports equipment, like Rawlings in the United States, so I was very happy to have my Tamanaco glove. It was like a prize. I would go outside with my father for a catch and feel like a professional baseball player with my fine new glove.

My arms were very long and this was good for throwing. For as far back as I can remember, I threw the ball hard. I was not so very strong but this did not matter when it came to throwing. My father taught me to throw the ball from the top, up high, with a snap of my wrist. Always down, down, down, from a high release point, like twelve o'clock on a watch. Even when I was little, I could see that this motion was very good for throwing. It gave me an advantage at shortstop because my throws to first base were strong and accurate. From the outfield, too, I could make a long throw to the catcher for a play at home plate. The other players knew to be careful when they were running against my arm. I do not know how my father understood about such things, because he was mostly a soccer player, but when you are an athlete you can see things in one sport even though you are accustomed to playing another. Anyway, it was good advice. Even today, when I am a professional pitcher, I can hear my father's voice telling me to throw the ball from the highest place.

Soon I heard people saying I had a very strong arm. It was not just my father or my friends saying this. It was not just the other players, knowing to be careful. It was other people, too. I only cared that they were saying something positive about how I played, that is all. In Caracas, and throughout Venezuela, there are many, many baseball people watching the games. Some of these people are the friends and family of the young players, but some are just baseball people, looking for the next famous big leaguer. They are not always scouts, working for major league teams. Sometimes they are just people who know baseball, men who like to be around the game, who take special pride in watching young players develop. None of these baseball men ever said anything about how I hit, or how I played in the field, because those things were just okay—they were nothing special, and so there was nothing to say. But now I started to think maybe my arm could be something special. One man who talked about me in this way was a coach named Henrique Riquezes. He knew a lot about baseball. He had an academy in Caracas where he trained young players. It was more like a little school than an academy. There were a lot of kids playing there, but the facilities were very basic, very simple. Henrique himself was nice, and professional, but his field was not so nice, not so professional. There was dirt where there should have been grass, and there were holes on the mound, but it did not matter so much because Henrique was a good teacher. He was very patient, very knowledgeable. He understood the game and what you needed to do to become a good player.

One day, when I was fifteen years old, Henrique told my father I could be a pitcher. He said this with great enthusiasm and invited me to join his academy. Up until this time, I had never really thought I could be a professional baseball player. It was something to dream about, like a perfect game, but it was not a realistic dream. There were so many players who were stronger, more talented, better trained. But now that a baseball man like Henrique Riquezes thought I could be a pitcher, I wanted very much to go to this academy, so my father made the arrangements. It did not cost any money. The agreement was that if I signed a professional contract we would give Henrique a certain amount. This was the agreement he had with all of his players. By now, Henrique has had about twenty of his students sign with a major league team. I am still the only one to make it to the major leagues, but back then no one had even been signed to a professional contract. Henrique was just starting out. We were taking a chance on him, the same way he was taking a chance on me.

My father and I, we did not care about such things. My mother, she cared only that it would not interfere with school. Her name is Maria, but everybody calls her Maritza. Pepe and Maritza, that is how my parents are known in our community. She was a chemistry teacher, so education was very important to her. I was not such a good student, but this did not matter. I could not play baseball in this academy if it interfered in any way with my education. This was her determination and I would have to go along with it.

I was very happy when I learned that I could go to baseball school and to regular school, both at the same time. Henrique's academy was near my house, so I would go there for practice each morning. I did not have to be in school until two o'clock. All of the kids my age went to school in the afternoon. It was a small school, and there was not enough room for all the students, so the younger kids would go to school in the morning and the older kids would go in the afternoon. This was very convenient because it allowed me to go to the baseball academy in the mornings. I would walk to the field and do my work there, and receive instruction from Henrique, and then I would go home and shower and continue to school.

It was a tiring routine, but this did not bother me because I was superhyper. I had a lot of energy, so for me this was a good schedule. Pitching at the academy gave me an ambition. Before, I was just playing, having fun. I was going to school. I do not think I gave a serious thought to what I would do after school, what kind of job I would like to have. I had never thought that I could have a job playing baseball. And now here I was, working every day with a baseball man who was telling me that I could maybe get signed by a professional team, if I worked hard and listened to what he had to say. This became my most important goal.

I was at the academy only a few weeks when I heard about a tryout. Some of the players were talking about it and making plans to go, so I asked Henrique if I could try out, too. I did not know how to do this. I did not know if you could just show up or if you had to register. I did not know if you could go without an invitation. I did not know anything.

But Henrique did not think this was such a good idea. I had only been pitching for a short time. He said, "It is too soon, Armando."

I said, "What does it matter? It is just for fun, to see how I can do."

He said, "No, it is not for fun. It is more serious than that. When the scouts see you, you have to be the best. If they do not like what they see the first time they see you, they will not look at you when you come back the next time, when you are ready."

I told my father about this tryout and he agreed with Henrique. He did not say that I was not ready, because I was his son and he thought I was a strong pitcher, but he believed it was a good idea to make a positive first impression. He believed we should follow Henrique. He said, "It is early, Armando. You have just started to practice. You are still learning."

And so I waited. For many weeks, I waited. The whole time I was waiting, I was working very hard. I did not mind the hard work because it had to do with baseball, and because it brought me closer to my goal. For me, this was better than school, more exciting, because it was preparing me for something I loved. Every morning, Henrique had a plan for me. He had a special plan for each of his players. Every plan started with running. At first I could not understand why I was running so much. Laps, sprints, all kinds of running. It was only later that I understood why running was so important: because to be a good pitcher you must be strong in your legs. Some days, after my running, Henrique had me work a bullpen session, practicing my breaking ball, my changeup, my fast ball. Before I started working with Henrique, I could not throw so many different pitches. I could only throw fast or slow. I did not know how to throw a curve ball, but Henrique taught me. I could not always throw it with very good control, but I was surprised at how much my ball could move. On other days, I worked on my fielding or my hitting.

We also played games. We did not always have enough players for two full teams, so Henrique had us playing different situations. If it was not our turn to pitch, we would be the base runners. Henrique would announce the situation—runner on first, two outs; bases loaded, nobody out—and then we would play. For pitchers, it was a way for us to rest our arms but still learn about everything that could happen on a baseball field. For the hitters and position players, it was also good practice.

I was making progress. I was not the best pitcher in Henrique's academy, and I was not the worst. I was in the middle. Every day I was learning something new. Every day I was looking forward to seeing my friends at the academy. Even the running I did not mind so much after a while. I would run with the other pitchers and we would talk about what it would be like to be professional baseball players. Together, we had something to dream about.

Finally, Henrique told me about another tryout. This one was for the Atlanta Braves, at their academy in Caracas. At that time, almost all of the major league teams had an academy in Venezuela. They were looking to sign a lot of players, so there was always a tryout marked on Henrique's calendar. He still did not think I was ready, but he now thought I was good enough to try. I could not believe how nice it was, this stadium where they had the tryout. It was not like the field at Henrique's academy. There was grass where there should be grass. There was dirt where there should be dirt and lines on the field where there should be lines on the field. It was like a palace for baseball. The only thing I had to complain about was that there were so many people, so many players. I did not think anyone would notice me. The other pitchers were all throwing the ball much harder than I could throw. They were bigger, stronger. I was only fifteen years old, and even though I was very tall I was also very skinny. These other players looked like men, and I just looked like a very tall, very skinny boy.

Oh, I was so nervous! I was sweating underneath my T-shirt.

When it was my turn to pitch, a man came over and told me what to do. I had been watching the other pitchers, so he did not really have to tell me. I could see that if the people running the tryout were not interested in you, they only asked you to make a few pitches. If they liked you, they asked you to keep throwing.

There were a lot of pitchers for them to see, so they had to be quick. They could not give everyone trying out the same number of pitches, but this was not always necessary. They could tell right away if they liked a pitcher, and I could tell, too, just by watching. This was one of the reasons why I was so nervous, because I worried that if I did not make a good pitch right away I would not get a chance to keep throwing.

And that is just what happened. I only threw about ten pitches before someone shouted, "Next!" So I had to admit that Henrique was right, but he was also right that it was a positive experience, because I promised myself that I would work even harder so I could be ready for my next tryout.

The next tryout came a short time later, after my sixteenth birthday. This time it was for Cleveland. I was now a little more prepared, a little bigger, a little stronger. Also, I was learning a new pitch, a slider. One of the coaches at Henrique's academy was teaching it to me. His name was Wilmer Ariscua. He never played professionally but he knew a lot about pitching. He could throw five or six different pitches, so there was always something new for him to teach me.

Anyway, I knew what to expect from this tryout. When it was my turn, I wanted to keep pitching. I did not want them to tell me to stop throwing after only ten pitches. The man running this tryout was a little different than the man running the Atlanta tryout. He started talking to me while I was on the mound. He said, "How old are you?" When I told him I was sixteen, he made a face like he could not believe it. He liked me, I could tell. Even before I threw my first pitch, I could tell.

He said, "You have a changeup?"

I nodded.

Whatever he asked me to throw, that is what I threw, and he started asking me some more questions. Like how long I have been pitching. Like if I had any brothers or sisters. Like how I was doing in school. I believe he wanted to get an idea of my character, my personality, to go along with an idea of my pitching. He said, "There is nice movement on your ball."

When I was finished, this first man took me to see another man who told me in Spanish that he wanted me to come back for another tryout the next week. It was a Tuesday or Wednesday, so I was anxious for the rest of the week to hurry up and be finished. This next tryout was to be at a different stadium, where some other scouts and coaches could see me pitch. If I did well, the second man said, Cleveland might sign me to a professional contract. He said, "Congratulations, Armando. You have a big future."

I was very happy when I left this tryout. No, I had not been signed to a professional contract, but there was now hope that I would be signed very soon. I was excited to go to this next tryout, but then something happened to change my plans. What happened was there was another tryout in between, this one for the Montreal Expos. Henrique found out about it and said we should go.

I said, "What about the people from Cleveland? They are expecting me at their tryout next week."

He said, "It will not hurt to go to this tryout first. You are not signed to Cleveland. Maybe you will be signed with Montreal instead."

My father thought this was practical. The promise of a contract is not a contract, he said. He agreed that I should go to as many tryouts as possible until I had a contract. In fact, my father was so happy about this tryout with Montreal that he arranged to take off from work to go with me. Henrique had a few other players he was bringing to this tryout. There were two shortstops and two other pitchers. We were all friends, because we were working and playing together every morning and sharing the same dream. We did not feel like we were competing with each other. We were helping each other and pushing each other and cheering for each other. We believed that if one of us could get signed, we all could get signed.

There were about twenty-five pitchers at this tryout but I was no longer so very nervous. I was not intimidated by the size of the other pitchers, or by their experience. I knew I had made a positive impression at the Cleveland tryout, so I did not put so much pressure on myself this time. It was like I had nothing to lose, so I was relaxed. There was an American scout named Fred Ferrera working for Montreal, and a local scout named Carlos Acosta. They were both very nice to me, very welcoming. I do not know why, but they seemed to be very interested in me. They had a radar gun, and I was throwing eighty-three, eighty-four. My velocity was very good, very consistent. I could see they were impressed.

One of them said, "Who brought you here today, Armando?"
I told them I was with my father and my coach, Henrique.

Fred Ferrera, the American, came over to shake my hand.
I remember thinking that the way he shook my hand was
unusual. Why? Because he squeezed so very hard. It was almost
painful, the way he was squeezing my hand. I did not know if he
was trying to see how strong I was, or if he was trying to judge
my reaction, or if this was just the way he shook hands. Finally,
he said, "We are interested in you, Armando. If you can wait
a few moments, we would like to talk to you and your father."

My heart did a leap in my chest when he said this but I tried
not to show it on my face. I wanted to smile, but I wanted to
keep it in, this smile. I did not think it would be good to show
my emotions, so I stepped away while they looked at another
few pitchers. I did my smiling on the inside.

When they were finished with their tryouts, my father and
I followed Fred Ferrera and Carlos Acosta to a small office.
There were two other pitchers following them, too. These other
pitchers went into the office first, one after the other. Then it
was our turn.

"Senor Galarraga," Fred Ferrera said, looking at my dad.
"We believe your son has potential. We would like to sign
him to a contract."

My father did not seem to care as much as I did about not
showing his emotions, because I could not remember a time
when I had seen him with such a big smile. He was so proud,
so happy.

The two men spoke mostly to my father. To them, I was
still a boy.

It was agreed that we would meet these two men the following day at a restaurant near the stadium to sign a contract. We did not ask about the money or the other matters to be discussed in the contract. All we cared about was that it was a contract. We did not even think about the other tryout we had scheduled for Cleveland, because that was only a hope. At first, it seemed like a promise, but now this promise from Montreal was a reality.

As we left the office, my father said, "Let's go to Grandpa's house and tell him the news. We'll get a beer and celebrate."

So we went to see my grandfather—my father's father. He was a big baseball fan, like us. He understood what it meant to sign a professional contract. We knew he would be excited by this news, and when we arrived at his door my father poked me in the ribs and said, "Tell him. Tell him."

It was a special moment for the men of my family. My grandfather was very happy for me when I told him my news. My father was even happier. I was very happy, too, but I do not think I was as happy as my father or my grandfather. I was as happy for them as I was for myself. In Venezuela, to be able to say your son or your grandson is a professional baseball player is a very fine thing. We sat at a table outside a small bodega, drinking our beers. It is unusual in Venezuela for a sixteen-year-old boy to drink beer with his father and grandfather, but this was a special celebration. This was an exception. Henrique was with us, and he was also happy. I was the first player from his academy to be signed by a major league team.

In the middle of our celebrating, my father said, "Do you think they're going to pay you, Armando? Or do we have to give you some money? I do not think we can afford so much, to send you away to play baseball."

This was how naive we were about professional baseball, how little we knew. Henrique knew a little more, of course. He said, "No, they will pay. Absolutely, they will pay him something when he signs the contract."

I said, "How much, do you think?"

No one could answer. No one could even guess, not even Henrique. Finally, my father took a sip of his beer and put his arm around me and said, "There is no use worrying. We will find out tomorrow."

The day after my tryout with Montreal, I went with my father to the restaurant to sign the contract. It was October 13, 1998—a most special day on our family calendar. The contract said that the Montreal Expos were going to pay me $3,500, in American dollars. It was a lot of money for 1998, for Venezuela. It was a lot of money for my family. It did not occur to us to ask for anything more.

Today, young players know to ask for as much as they can get. They know to tell one team if another team is interested. But I only cared that these people liked the way I pitched, and that I would now have a chance to pitch in the major leagues. Maybe not right away, but there was now a chance. This was payment enough.

I did not stop to think about what it meant to sign for the Montreal Expos. I had only heard a little bit about Montreal. I had not seen many games for the Expos. They were not one of the most famous teams in Venezuela. They did not have a lot of famous players, except for Vladimir Guerrero. He was from the Dominican Republic. They did not have so many players from Venezuela. And they were all the way away, in Canada, so it was not so easy to see their games or know their players.

Also, the Montreal Expos did not have a special uniform or a special personality, like my favorite American team, the Oakland A's. I liked their white shoes. It is another funny thing that seven years later, in 2007, I would finally make my major league debut in Oakland, against my favorite American team. It was like the connection I had with Ken Griffey Jr. I had always cheered for Oakland. I liked their green and yellow jerseys. I liked Rickey Henderson and Ruben Sierra and Jose Canseco. They were very good players, very popular players. And Dennis Eckersley. He was a very good relief pitcher.

And so, no, the Montreal Expos were not my favorite American team, and they were certainly not my very favorite team of all, *Leones del Caracas*. They did not play in the *Liga Venezolana de Béisbol Profesional*. But now they were *my* team. They took an interest in me so now I would take an interest in them. Now I would root for them. They gave me a hat. They gave me some T-shirts. So now I was able to walk around Caracas like a Montreal Expo, and I did so with great pride and a feeling of belonging. I could close my eyes and count how long it would take before I would be in Canada, helping my new teammates win a championship.

My mother was very proud of me when she heard about the $3,500 but she worried what it meant for me and school. She understood about baseball, of course. She knew what an accomplishment it was to receive a professional contract. But she also knew that I was still a long way from a successful career. It was important to her that I finish high school. There was nothing certain about baseball, she said. The only thing certain was my education. My mother was very firm about this. She was not rooting for me to fail as a player, but she wanted me to be prepared in case I did not find the success I was looking for. She said I could not go away to play rookie ball until I finished high school. She was a teacher, so she made the necessary arrangements. She knew of a place where adults who had not finished high school could graduate on a very fast schedule. In the United States, they have these kinds of programs all over the country, but in Venezuela they are not so common.

The arrangement she made was that I could go to this other school for adults. I was only sixteen years old, with a little more than a year and a half until I finished high school, but now I had to finish all my courses in just a few months before my mother would allow me to play rookie ball. It was very difficult because I was not always such a good student, but I did not mind working hard for this goal because it meant I could play baseball. The other students in this program were much older. Some of them were the age of my parents. They looked at me like I was just a baby, but I was able to keep up with them on the tests. One week, I had an important test every single day, and then on top of all those tests I was playing baseball in the mornings, so I was always very tired. I was always feeling a lot of pressure. I had to remember math, chemistry, history, *Castellano*, English . . . so many different subjects. It felt to me like my head would explode with everything I had to remember, but I would not let that happen.

When I was frustrated, I would say, "Mom, why do I have to take all these classes?"

But then she would explain why it was so important, in case I did not go very far in professional baseball. A lot of players, they never get past rookie ball, she reminded me. "That will not be you, Armando," she would say, "but you must be prepared."

And so I prepared.

It was another happy day when I graduated from this special school. All of my friends had another year or more of high school, but now I was ready to begin my baseball career. This was the agreement I had made with my mother, so as soon as possible my parents drove me to Valencia, which was where the summer league team for Montreal was based. It was about a three-hour drive from my home and I could not wait for the miles to pass so I could start playing.

I cannot be certain but I think I wore my Montreal Expos hat the whole way there.

Toledo

My story is a lot like Armando's, but it's the flip side of the dream because it didn't exactly work out for me as a player. It's me thinking from the start I'd pitch well enough in high school to get drafted by a big league club. It's me going on to college and not really getting a good look by the pro scouts, even though I had a decent enough career, and then licking my wounds and finding a kind of back door to keep me in the game.

Wasn't cut out for anything else but baseball, really. Or maybe I was but couldn't think what that anything else might be.

Kinda weird that we wound up on the same field, me and Armando, doing our thing. That we were thrown together in Detroit, of all places. Actually, the connection reaches all the way to Toledo, Ohio. That's where I'm from, born and raised, and by some crazy twist of baseball fate that's where Armando Galarraga started his 2010 baseball season, pitching for the Toledo Mud Hens, the Triple-A affiliate of the Detroit Tigers.

Baseball is like that sometimes. You keep coming up with all these overlapping circles. A reporter told me about this Toledo connection, and at first I thought it was a little freaky, but then I just thought, *Hey, that's baseball.* It all ties in.

So here's the story of my baseball career. First, a little background: I grew up a die-hard Yankees fan, even though the Tigers and Indians were each less than an hour away. Weren't too many Yankees fans on my street, I'll say that. Wasn't so easy to follow an out-of-town team, I'll say that, too. You could follow your local team on television and radio, and then on Saturdays you could watch the game of the week, or maybe you'd catch the highlights from around the league on *This Week in Baseball.* That was it, and it just so happened that when I came of age as a baseball fan the Yankees were still winning everything. I was born in 1955, so when I started watching games the Yankees were the team to beat. Mickey Mantle, Roger Maris, Yogi Berra, Whitey Ford, Tom Tresh . . . all those guys. They were my first heroes.

For some reason, I don't remember ever making it to Tiger Stadium to see the Yankees play. We could only afford to go once or twice each year, but those Yankees series were always sold-out. Couldn't get near those tickets. Every year, my dad tried. Every year, we circled those games on the schedule but never made it. We were disappointed, but only a little. We still made it out to the stadium. I remember going to see the Twins a couple times, and the White Sox, but I couldn't bring myself to root for the Tigers. No, sir. Most people, they grow up in Toledo, they root for the Tigers or the Indians. It's split right down the middle, only not in my house. Even those

great Tigers teams of the 1960s, with Al Kaline and Denny
McLain, Jim Northrup, and Norm Cash couldn't turn me into
a fan. They went to the World Series in 1968 and I was old
enough to appreciate good baseball so, of course, I watched all
those games, but I wasn't one of those bandwagon kids who
could just start rooting for whatever team was playing well.
The Yankees, that was my team. Took a lot of heat for it as a
kid, but that didn't bother me. I knew what I knew.

Guess there was a lot of disappointment with me and baseball. Guess it's like a running theme. Goes back to rooting for
the Yankees, in a way, because when all my friends were going
crazy over the Tigers in the World Series, the Yankees were
lousy. Seemed like they were last or next-to-last every year.
They took a lot of heat for this, too—but hey, that's baseball.

Probably, it goes back even further, the game breaking my
heart. First time my dad took me to try out for a team, they
turned me away. I was only eight years old, and you had to be
nine to play in this one league, but the folks in charge didn't
say anything at first. I was out there warming up, tossing the
ball around, and then one of the coaches came over and told
my dad I couldn't play because I was too young. Just about
crushed me, but those were the rules. Had to wait a whole year
before I could try out again and I thought those days would
never pass on the calendar. I can still taste what that feels like,
waiting for a shot to do something you love, thinking you'll
never get there.

By the time I got my chance to play, I was good and ready.
Back then, we played for our grade school. It was like Little
League, except you represented your school, so I played for

St. John's. We had two teams: the Orioles and the Cardinals. I was assigned to the Orioles, and I can still close my eyes and picture our green and yellow uniforms. Wasn't anything like the pinstripes of my New York Yankees, but I was pretty damn proud of that first uniform. Made me feel like a ballplayer, at long last. I think I walked around the house for weeks in that thing. My mom had to peel it off me.

Like a lot of kids, my dad got me into baseball. He was James A. Joyce Jr., so I'm the third. My son is also a James, but we changed his middle name so he can start the string all over again. Most people, they catch my name, they make some comment about James Joyce, the writer. For a long time, we used to think we were related, in a distant way, but my son has a degree in history and he's been looking into it, researching the Joyce family tree back in Ireland, and he's point-blank determined there's no relation at all. Wish I'd known that, growing up. Wouldn't have felt such pressure to read *Ulysses* back in high school. My son, he wouldn't have felt the same pressure.

My daughter Keri always says she's lucky to escape the name. Means she never had to go through these same motions— because *Ulysses* is one tough nut to crack. Even took a class on it in college. My dad couldn't get through it, either, and he was a big reader. Craziest thing about that book is there's a whole chapter that's just one sentence. It's the longest sentence in the English language, so how are you supposed to make sense of that?

It's still on my "bucket list" of things to do in this life, get through that book. I'll get around to it, eventually. That's my attitude about most everything. If it takes me a time or two to figure something out, I'll stick with it until that time or two is done. Even if it means finding my way through some back door when I can't make it through the front.

My brother Tim never had that pressure, to read that book, to live up to that name. He's four years younger than me, and we were cut a little differently. He played ball for a couple years when we were kids, but he never really took to it. He loves the game, knows his sports inside and out, but he wasn't such a serious athlete. He was into his own thing, so baseball became something we could all share as fans, as a family, even though it was also something for just me and my dad. We had the same name, the same passion for playing, so it was a kind of glue for us, you could say.

Baseball is like that, too, you know. It binds people together. Hang around the game long enough and you'll see that in a big-time way.

Wasn't a whole lot of time for my dad to play ball with me and my brother. Not during the week, at least. He was like a lot of dads in my neighborhood in those days. He worked in the automobile industry. Toledo was a big car town. Still is, of course. There was a Jeep factory. It started out as Willy's Overland Jeep, and then it switched to Kaiser Jeep, and then American Motors Jeep. Eventually it became Chrysler Jeep, and that's where my dad worked, for thirty-two years. He retired from Chrysler with a nice pension. He was the guy in the payroll department who took care of all the time clocks and kept track of everyone's hours.

He used to play catch with me at night and on the weekends. Not because he had to but because he wanted to. He was a payroll guy so he punched a clock same as everyone else. He could never cut out early but when his shift was through he hurried home to be with us kids. That was always a big thing, depending on the time of year, to catch whatever daylight was left so we could throw the ball around a bit before dinner. And then, when I started playing, he set it up so he could make it to most of my games.

Turned out I was a decent pitcher. I was a good athlete all around, but I had a talent for pitching. Even drew some scouts down to Central Catholic in Toledo, where I played high school ball. Truth be told, it might have been just one scout, but in those days most teams used a kind of central scouting bureau, so one was enough. That was the first time someone put it in my head that I could play professionally. That is, someone other than me. Back of my mind, I'd had that same thought for myself, going back to when I first put on that green and yellow Orioles uniform, but to hear it from coaches and scouts and other baseball people . . . well, that was something.

Ended up going to college on a scholarship to Bowling Green State University, in Bowling Green, Ohio. We played in the Mid-American Conference, against schools like Ohio University, Miami of Ohio, Ball State. We were a notch or two below those powerhouse collegiate programs, but we were competitive. Game to game, we could play with those guys.

In fact, during my time at school, we sent one Mid-American school all the way to the finals of the College World Series in 1976—Eastern Michigan University. They lost to Arizona, the last time a team from one of the northern states made it all the way to the finals. That Eastern Michigan team had a killer pitching staff, led by Bob Owchinko and Bob Welch, who both went on to nice major league careers.

One of my Bowling Green teammates made it all the way to the bigs—Larry Owen, my roommate. We all called him Buck, and he hung on for a bunch of years as a backup catcher for the Braves and the Royals. I got to thinking that all these guys I knew were getting drafted, getting signed, all these guys I was playing against, so it would just be a matter of time before I had my shot, too. I had a strong, live arm, and pitched pretty well my first couple years, but then I hurt my foot during my junior year. Not to make excuses or anything, but it cost me some momentum, some attention. What happened was I developed a ganglion cyst on the top of my foot and had to have it removed, but the operation went bad. Came down with a staph infection, ended up missing a bunch of time, and when my senior year came around I was just getting back to form. Wound up having a solid season but it was one of those too little, too late situations.

I still remember the last game of my college career. First game of a doubleheader, at Kent State, about a hundred miles from home. I got into trouble in the seventh inning, which was supposed to be my last inning. At that time, when we played doubleheaders, the games were only seven innings long, so I was determined to finish what I'd started. Thought I'd end my college career on a high note. We were up 2–1 and I walked the lead-off hitter, which of course was not what I wanted to do in that situation. My coach, Don Purvis, didn't look too happy about it, so I tried a little too hard to pick this guy off first, ended up throwing the ball away and allowing the runner to advance to second. Again, not what I wanted to happen.

At this point, runner on second, nobody out, Coach Purvis came out to talk to me. I was never a big fan of those trips to the mound. Always felt like I was being taken out to the tool shed in front of the whole world. But I was always respectful, always gave the coach my full attention.

He said, "Jimmy, I've got nobody left in the pen. We've got another game right after this one. It's all on you."

Turned out I couldn't keep that runner on second from scoring but I held Kent State to that one run, and then our guys came back and put another run on the board in the top of the eighth to make it 3–2, and that's how it ended. Wasn't exactly the high note I was reaching for, but it was high enough, so I came off the field feeling pretty good.

Well, that good feeling lasted just a couple hours because Coach Purvis wanted to give us his end-of-season evaluations before the bus ride back to campus, so after the second game we were all hanging around the field for that to happen. Took a long time, waiting on Coach to get to everybody, but I didn't mind. It was our last piece of business, and I was hoping to hear some encouragement, some ideas of what I might do next.

When my turn came, Coach Purvis came up to me and said, "I don't think you're gonna make it. You don't have the stuff."

It was late on a Saturday afternoon and I was a long way from home, and an even longer way from where I wanted to be. Wasn't expecting to hear something like this, but Coach was matter-of-fact about it. Had me thinking I was done. In all fairness to him, he was a good guy stuck in a tough spot, delivering some bad news, and I guess he thought the best way to do it was quick and straightforward, no bullshit. Said the same thing to a lot of the other guys on the team, so it was a miserable bus ride back to campus for us seniors. It was right around graduation and most of us hadn't thought of anything but baseball, so it was a hell of a time to have to regroup.

Me, I hadn't exactly planned ahead. It helps to remember that in those days the amateur baseball draft wasn't the only draft on the minds of young players. Wasn't even the most important. For a long time, there was also the military draft to consider. Mercifully, by the time I graduated, in 1977, the war in Vietnam was finally over so I didn't have to worry about losing my college exemption. Truth was, I hadn't had to worry about it all through my first four years of school, but I worried about it anyway. We all did, back then. The year I graduated high school, I was still only seventeen, but my draft number came in at #3. Didn't really matter just yet, but it caught my attention. The next year, when I'd turned eighteen, it came in at #365, which was a whole lot better. Still didn't matter, because I was in school, but it was the kind of thing you carried with you at the time. It stamped you, going forward.

I had a couple cousins who'd served in Vietnam so the idea of going over and fighting for my country might have been something to think about, and even though the war was officially over I suppose I could have enlisted and served in one way or another, but I wasn't ready to let go of baseball just yet. There was a tryout a couple weeks away, in Jackson, Michigan, which was only about a forty-five-minute drive from my house in Toledo. The Cincinnati Reds used to stage a bunch of these tryouts throughout the area, mostly for high school kids to come out and show their stuff. They were real cattle calls. In fact, I don't think I knew anyone who got a good, fair look at one of these things. It was just a way for teams to make sure they were covering all the bases, to make sure no good young player was missed. I decided to head out to Jackson to see if I had enough pop in my arm to turn a couple heads.

Unfortunately, I didn't get to throw a single pitch. The try-out was rained out, and I took it as a sign. Figured it was the end of the road for me and baseball, and I drove back to Toledo wondering what my life might look like punching a clock down at the Jeep plant, same as my dad. My mother was there, too, so I'd be keeping up the family tradition. She did line work, helping to build luggage racks, so I'd have an edge on all those other recent graduates looking for work, the ones with only one parent working at the factory. Plus, I'd worked there every summer since high school, so I knew the drill. And I knew my cars. That part of the world, you don't know your cars, you don't know spit. Some of my friends, they could tell you the make and model of any car coming down the street from the rumble of the engine. Not me, though. I needed a good look, too.

My first car? A 1964 Ford Galaxy XL 500. Gray, four-door, red interior. Used to call it "The Bullet." My dad bought it for me when I was a junior in high school, and the deal was I had to drive my mom to work each morning on my way to school. Not such a bad trade. And it was just a one-way deal, because I was always playing some sport or other after school, so my mom found another way home.

I never really minded working at Jeep when it was just a summer job. When you're still in school and working at the plant, it's just a way to earn some extra money. You wear those grease stains like a badge. When you're out of school, and out of ideas as a ballplayer, it's a dead end. Those grease stains are just stains. That's the attitude I took with me to the plant, first day of work. They put me on the assembly line, gave me a grease gun, and told me to grease the tie rods. Eight hours a day, $4.15 an hour. Huge money at the time, and I should have been thrilled to land such a good, steady job, but I felt defeated. There were a whole bunch of union benefits that kicked in after ninety days, which I might have paid attention to, but I didn't think I could make it ninety days. In fact, I was so sure this was just a temporary gig I didn't pay any attention to that union stuff.

Wasn't through with baseball, I guess.

I should probably backtrack a bit. All the way back to when I was sixteen years old, to my first "real" job with the recreation department of the city of Toledo, calling balls and strikes for youth baseball games. Wasn't a whole lot of training: if you knew the game, you were qualified.

I worked as an umpire for only one season, until my summer Jeep job kicked in. My immediate supervisor at the recreation department was a guy named Tom Ravashire. Tom had spent a bunch of years bouncing around the minors, first as a player in the Dodgers organization and later as an umpire. He was one of those rough, tough, gruff, take-no-prisoners types, like an umpire sent from central casting. He used to sit with a group of us after games, spinning war stories. Baseball war stories. I remember being amazed at his ability to recall all these great details. The score, the count, the runners on base . . . Tom had been umpiring a long while at this point, and there were stories from every stop along the way. Baseball stories, at bottom, but he told them like an umpire and I heard them like a player, and somewhere in between he made me feel like these crappy diamonds in the middle of these crappy towns were just about the most magical places on God's green earth.

After a couple weeks greasing tie rods, I decided to stop by the rec office to see if Tom was still around. Hadn't been in touch with him in four or five years, but I thought he'd be a good guy to talk to about some kind of next move. I was bored over at Jeep, itching for something else. And I was probably a little depressed at the way my baseball career had come to such a sudden end. Back of my mind, I'd been thinking of umpiring as a way to get back in the game. I still thought I could play, but there wasn't anyone about to give me a shot, so this was one way to keep baseball in my life.

Tom was happy to see me. Said he remembered me. Said he'd followed my college career. Don't know if either of these things was even close to true, but I was happy to hear them. I told Tom I was thinking of getting into umpiring, and he set me straight. Told me what was involved, what to expect. Said the chances of making it all the way to the bigs were slim to none, but it would be a hell of a ride. "Either you love it or you don't," he said. "Either you're cut out for this kind of life or you're not."

I decided right then and there that I would and that I was.

First things first: I went home and told my parents about an umpiring school Tom had mentioned called Umpire Development, run by a guy named Barney Deary down in Florida. I sent away for a brochure. The school had changed since Tom's last dealings with them and was now called the Bill Kinnamon School of Umpiring. It cost about $2,000 to attend, for a five-week session, and at that time it was one of the only programs that fed umpires directly into the professional ranks. I also found in the *Sporting News* a listing for another umpiring school run by Harry Wendelstedt that was said to offer a decent pipeline to the bigs, but Tom said Kinnamon's school was the best so it was the only place I really looked.

My parents didn't think I was serious when I laid it out for them. For one thing, they didn't think I could come up with the $2,000 tuition, which was a whole lot of money back then, and a whole lot more than I had lying around, but they also didn't think umpiring was any kind of career. My dad had worked a bunch of years calling youth games in and around Toledo, but it was only a sideline gig for him. In his mind, it was more like a hobby than a job. All along, my parents had pretty much left me alone when it came to plans for my future, but I'm sure they thought about it. I've got kids of my own now, at that same stage of life—so, yeah, absolutely, they were thinking about it. Probably kept them up nights, me being so uncertain, so unfocused with what I wanted to do. Like I said, I'd only ever wanted to be a professional baseball player. Hadn't planned for anything else. So when they thought about it at all, my folks probably thought I'd hang in there at Jeep, or maybe wind up in coaching or teaching, because my degree was in education. But umpiring? Had to be the furthest thing from their minds. Still, they didn't push me one way or another. They just heard me out and told me it was my call.

Now, as I mentioned, there was a time when my father had his own romantic notions about umpiring. He used to have beers with a guy named Joe Amborski, a fixture on the local umpiring scene. Same way I used to sit and listen to Tom Ravashire, my father used to sit and listen to Joe. They were great storytellers, with great stories to tell, and one day Joe started telling my dad how they always needed new umpires to help call local youth games. That's all it was, really. My father had always been crazy for baseball, spent all that time throwing the ball around with me and my brother and taking us to games, so he signed up. They gave him a blue shirt and he was an umpire. Worked a couple games a week, evenings and weekends. Didn't need the extra cash or anything. Said he did it for beer money and for something to do.

I used to go and watch my dad work some of these games, only I was in high school by this point so I was mostly inter-ested in the game itself. I didn't really care that it was my dad calling balls and strikes behind the plate. That part got old pretty quick. Got old for him, too. He didn't really have the stomach for the way people turned on him when they didn't like a call. I remember one game, with fourteen-year-olds, when there was a close play at the plate and one side didn't particularly care for my father's call. That's how it happens on a close play. One side thinks you're blind, and one side thinks you've got the wisdom of Solomon. But this time it got ugly. The players and parents on the wrong side of the call followed my dad to the parking lot after the game, harassing him the whole way to his car, and he gave it up soon after that. He said, "I'm not gonna take that kind of crap."

Can't imagine my folks thought I was serious about giving up a good union job at Jeep. Most likely, they heard me out and dismissed it as a phase, a passing interest. I was on my own in this, so I started saving like crazy, picking up extra shifts when I could, holding back on expenses. I gave myself a deadline: end of January 1978, the same deadline I'd need to meet for my application. I'd started full-time at Jeep in July 1977, and six months seemed like enough time to save $2,000. Plus, the next Bill Kinnamon session started up in February, just before spring training. The idea was if you did well in umpire school, you'd have a shot at a job at one of the minor league spring training camps, and possibly hire on in the low level minors for the coming season. I didn't want to have to wait a whole other year for the next opportunity to come around on the calendar.

Finally, the deadline came and I had enough money saved so I sent in my deposit. Then I gave notice at Jeep and made plans to drive to Florida. The Bullet had been retired by this point, in favor of a 1975 Buick LeSabre custom convertible. Burgundy. So I drove down to St. Petersburg, Florida, in style, and I pulled into the Kinnamon complex thinking, *Okay,*

Jimmy. One way or another, you're getting into professional base-ball. That was my attitude. There were about a hundred of us, and we were all cut the same way. We were all in our early to mid twenties. We were all disappointed athletes, brick-walled a little too soon in one sport or other. Right out of the gate, they said about a third of us would compete for spots at the next level, which was like an umpiring finishing school, and that half of that group would move up the ranks and actually land a professional job. The bottom third wouldn't even make it through the five-week program.

Keep in mind, I still hadn't given up entirely on the idea of playing professional baseball. I had my mitt in the back of the car. I had my spikes. I had everything. I even called my old roommate Larry Owen, told him I was coming down to Florida to go to umpire school and asked him if there was any chance he could arrange a tryout for me with the Atlanta Braves. He'd just played a season of rookie ball and was probably going to start the 1978 season in A ball, but I thought he had some kind of in.

He didn't.

The Kinnamon school was run on a Little League complex in St. Petersburg. There were four fields, in pretty decent shape, and a couple of barracks. There were about thirty or forty of us crammed into each building, on bunk beds. The rest were commuters. There was also a giant classroom, where we sat for lectures and courses. The way they had it set up, we'd do rule book work in the morning and field work in the afternoon. After four weeks, they sent us out to work games—high school, junior college, whatever they could fit into our schedules—and we'd be evaluated. If we did well, we'd move up the road to Bradenton, where the top candidates from the Kinnamon school would combine with the top candidates from the Wendelstedt school for an intensive two-week session, competing for about ten to fifteen spots as minor league umpires coming out of spring training.

First day of class, soon as they laid out these numbers for us, I told myself I'd finish in one of those top spots. There was no doubt in my mind, which probably sounds a little arrogant but that's the mind-set you needed to get ahead in this group. Most of us were hard-chargers, with aggressive personalities. You don't see too many shy and retiring umpires, so you had to have a certain confidence, a certain swagger. Not just in the classroom but out on the field. You needed to carry yourself as a kind of authority.

Just to give you an idea, about three-quarters of the guys who can't cut it in umpiring school wind up working in law enforcement, so there's definitely something to this swagger. One way or another, we're drawn to positions of authority. One field or another, we like to be in charge.

We'd start our field work sessions by playing catch. It was a good way to loosen up for the running around we'd have to do, but it was also a good way for the major league umpires running the sessions to see who could play and who couldn't. They didn't want to put someone at first base who couldn't catch the ball. Most times, they got it right.

Usually, I'd stand in as a pitcher because I could throw it over the plate and jump-start whatever drill they'd have us run. There was a kid in the program we all called Bama, because that's where he was from, and he had a cannon of an arm, so he always played third. One afternoon, for whatever reason, the instructors put a kid over at first who couldn't catch a throw across the diamond from a guy like Bama. Sure enough, one of the first plays of the day, Bama fired to first and hit this poor kid right in the nose. He went down like he'd been shot. There was blood everywhere. Kid's face blew up like you wouldn't believe. We were running drills on two different fields at the time, and everything just stopped. Had to send someone running back to the office to call 911. We all huddled around this poor kid, thinking maybe Bama had killed him. Really, the kid wasn't moving, but then the ambulance came and the EMT guys started working on him, got him on a gurney and took him to the hospital. Next day, he showed up at school for classroom work first thing in the morning, looking like a raccoon, but he didn't miss a day. That's the kind of single-minded focus and sense of purpose you needed to make it through this program.

Sure enough, I was one of the guys tapped for Bradenton. I was excited, but not too excited. Still wasn't where I wanted to be. Still had to finish at the top of this next group to get a minor league job. (By the way, the kid with the busted nose didn't make the cut.)

At Bradenton, our expenses were covered. There were about thirty of us at this point, and the routine was a lot like it was at the School of Umpiring, only here we were working more games, with more talented players, alongside better student-umpires. That's how it goes with umpiring. You've got to be sharper, more focused, more knowledgeable at each level of the game. Tom Ravashire can get away with hiring a high school kid who knows baseball to call balls and strikes for a youth league game back in Toledo, but when you start working minor league spring training games you need to know your stuff.

Turned out, I did. Made enough of an impression to get assigned to the Chicago White Sox minor league spring training camp in Sarasota, Florida. Now I was getting excited, because now I was on my way—just a couple months after starting umpiring school. And I was getting paid. Not a lot of money, mind you. Nothing like I'd be making at Jeep, but a couple hundred bucks for the run of spring training, plus five dollars a day in meal money. They also put us up, in another barracks close to the spring training complex.

In Sarasota, I was assigned to a crew made up of an umpire from Triple A, an umpire from Double A, and two "apprentice" umps from Bradenton. For these few weeks, we were considered A-ball umps but we were still vying for jobs out of spring training. We were still auditioning, still being evaluated, so we tended to move around like someone was always watching us, even off the field—because, basically, someone always was.

Pregame

ARMANDO GALARRAGA

Rinoceronte

I do not like to talk too much before a game when I am pitching. I like to be by myself, away from my teammates. Some pitchers, they are more relaxed, they joke around in the clubhouse, but that is not my way. That is not my focus. Before a game, I talk to the catcher. I talk to the pitching coach. That is all. Together, we come up with a plan for the game. Together, we talk about our approach. This guy, we might want to pitch away, away. This guy, he likes to run when he is on base. This guy, he is aggressive with two strikes.

All through the lineup, this is what we talk about, but not right before the game. This happens a few hours before, when we get to the stadium. It can take ten minutes or it can take an hour, depending on who is the catcher and who is the other team and what we are planning. But right before the game, I am by myself. If we are in the dugout, waiting to go onto the field, I am at the far end of the bench, away from everyone else. I am thinking, concentrating. And it does not begin the day of the game, my concentration. It begins just after my last start. It begins in a small way, and then it gets bigger. I look to see who I am facing, where we are playing. I listen to my body, to my arm. I rest. I throw. I rest. I focus. Everything else besides baseball, I try to push away from my thinking. I do this more and more, until it is my turn to pitch again, when I do this most of all.

All during the season, I try to keep this focus, to keep my thoughts clear, but the day before I am going to pitch, if we are facing the same opponent, I will pay attention to the lineup. I will see how they do against the other pitchers on my team.

Finally, when it is my turn to pitch, I look a little more closely at the hitters on the other team. Tonight, I am thinking a lot about Shin-Soo Choo, the Cleveland outfielder. He is a good hitter, a dangerous hitter. He is the one I am thinking about the most because he is the one who gives me the most problems. He does not always hit against other pitchers, but against me he can always hit. The last time I pitched against the Indians, he hit a ground-rule double to deep left field to drive in the first run of the game. There are other big hitters playing for Cleveland, like Travis Hafner, but I do not worry about them the same way I worry about Shin-Soo Choo. He is a good player but he is not a big player, but to me his name in the lineup looks like Albert Pujols.

I do not look too much at the numbers when I look at the other team's lineup, because they only tell you what has happened in the past. They will not tell you what will happen next. Instead, I look at who is playing well, who is hitting the ball hard, who is having good at bats. This is different than looking at the batting averages. Yes, it is also about the past, but it is only about the very recent past, so it can come a little closer to what will happen next. It is a better place to start than to look back at the whole season. It is better to just look back at the last game, the last series.

When I warm up before a game, I do not throw the ball too hard. I only try to get loose. I do not throw more than 60 or 70 percent. Even on my last pitch. I do not want to show the other team everything I have. Sometimes, before a game, I leave the bullpen after warming up and feel like I will pitch a shutout. My arm is strong. My control is very good. And then I will start the game and my fastball will not be so fast, my control not so good. Other times, it is the opposite. Other times, I do not feel so strong and then in the first inning the hitters cannot touch me. And so here is what I have learned: you never know. It is a simple lesson but it took me a long time to learn it. It took many disappointments and many surprises for me to learn that all you can do is prepare and focus and hope to pitch well.

Here is an example: in my rookie season, 2008, with the Detroit Tigers, there was a game in Kansas City when I did not feel so strong as I was warming up. I did not have such good control and there was no movement on my fastball. Brandon Inge was the catcher and he came to talk to me before I threw my first pitch. He could see that I was not very confident, that I did not believe I would have a good game, so he was trying to cheer me up. He said, "Don't worry, Gala. It will come."

And so you see, you never know how you will do before a game begins. You can think you know, but you will never really know. You can think you are about to pitch the worst game of your career, and then after a few pitches you start to think it will be the best game of your career. That is just what happened at this game in Kansas City, only not right away. Even after the first inning, I did not feel so confident. There was a soft line drive to shortstop, a soft ground ball back to me, and a soft fly ball to right field. Three up, three down, and they could only hit the ball soft, soft, soft. But even after such a good start, I did not think I was pitching my best, so you can see this is always a very big mystery for a pitcher, a very big question mark.

And here is the rest of that story: in the second inning, I started to feel more confident, more in control, and every inning it was the same. Three up, three down. All the way through six innings. After the fourth inning, the Kansas City fans were yelling to me that I had a no-hitter. In baseball, you are not sup-posed to talk about a no-hitter when it is happening because it is considered bad luck, but the fans did not care. They were for the home team, and I was for the visiting team, and they were yelling for me to have bad luck. But I am not a superstitious person so it did not bother me. It gave me motivation, to keep pitching a no-hitter, but in the seventh inning the designated hitter David DeJesus led off with a single, so that was the end of the perfect game. He ended up scoring the only run of the game for Kansas City, but that was the end of my good luck for that one game. However, it was an important game for me because it showed everyone that I could be a dominant pitcher. And it was important for me, too, because it showed that I could have a bad warm-up and still have a good game.

Tonight, my focus is not only on this one game against Cleveland. It is on my whole season. Also, it is on my whole career, because my season did not start the way I wanted, and because the season before did not finish the way I wanted. Before the 2009 season, my manager Jim Leyland said that the only pitchers with a guarantee to make the starting rotation were me and Justin Verlander. This was a special thing for me to hear. He said this about Justin Verlander because he is a great pitcher. He said this about me because I had a very good year in 2008. It was not only that one start in Kansas City. It was the whole season. I was one of the leaders for rookie of the year. I was one of the leaders in earned run average. I won thirteen games. Everybody said it was a very promising start for my career, so it is a long way to go from so much success to so much struggle. I went from one of the league leaders in 2008 and one of the important parts in the Detroit rotation going into 2009 to someone who could not even make the team in 2010 coming out of spring training.

My struggles, they did not happen right away. I continued to have success at the start of the 2009 season. I started our first game at home, which was a very great honor. And I pitched a good game: seven innings, five hits, one run. We won by a big score against the Texas Rangers, 15–2, so I was very happy. For all of my starts in April 2009, I was happy. I was 3–0, with a 1.85 ERA, but then my arm began to hurt and my delivery changed. After April, my record was 3–10, so you can see what happened. You can also see that I finished the season in the bullpen, as a reliever. I did not like this very much but I could not complain because I did not give the Tigers many reasons to keep me in the rotation. I could not always throw my fastball for a strike or find a way to get hitters out.

The sportswriters and announcers have a saying for this. They say that a pitcher "pitched himself out of the rotation." For many years, I heard this saying but they were never talking about me. Now I heard this saying, on ESPN, and they were talking about me. Now it meant something different. It was very upsetting to know that you were once one of two pitchers the manager liked enough to promise a place in the rotation even before spring training, and now you were only an extra arm for the bullpen.

And so, here in 2010, I believed once again that I had to prove myself. I believed this because this was what they told me when I did not make the team after spring training. They sent me to Toledo instead. They said they were still counting on me to be a big part of the team but they had a lot of starters and they wanted me to get back to how I was pitching in 2008. I did not like this decision but I could not complain. I could only go to Toledo and work hard and hope to pitch well, so this was what I did, and after a few starts I was back in Detroit, back in the rotation.

Already I had made two starts, a very good start against Boston and a not so good start in an interleague game against Los Angeles. After the not so good start, I was in the bullpen, but then something happened to put me back in the rotation. The Tigers traded Dontrelle Willis to Arizona. It happened only yesterday, less than twenty-four hours before I am throwing my first warm-up pitch. Dontrelle was one of our starting pitchers, but the sportswriters were saying the same thing about him that they said last year about me, that he was pitching his way out of the rotation, so now that he was traded it meant there was a new chance for me to pitch my way back into the rotation. In baseball, for somebody to move up, somebody has to move down. It is the way of the game. Everybody told me Dontrelle Willis's job as the fifth starter would be for me, so you can see there is an extra pressure to do well. But I tell myself I cannot worry about this now. I can only worry about the game, about the Cleveland lineup, about my approach.

These are the things I am trying not to think about as I step to the mound for my final warm-up. In the front of my thinking there is only the game and the approach I have discussed with my catcher, Alex Avila, and my pitching coach, Rick Knapp. There is only the Cleveland batter Shin-Soo Choo, who gives me the most problems. But then in the back there is the whole rest of my baseball life. There is me trying to show manager Jim Leyland that I belong in the rotation, now that there is an empty spot. There is me trying to get back to how I pitched in my rookie season.

For my last warm-up pitch I throw a fastball but I do not put everything on it. I am at about 70 percent in my velocity, and 70 percent in my control. I do not feel like I am at my best, and I do not feel like I am at my worst. I am fifty-fifty, somewhere in the middle. I can dominate or struggle or just do okay. There is no way for me to know.

I step off the mound and turn around while Alex Avila throws down to second base. It is a baseball tradition, before the start of every inning, for the catcher to throw to second base after the final warm-up pitch, but I do not pay attention. Instead, I have my own tradition. It is like a superstition, only I am not superstitious so I call it a tradition. I take off my hat and look inside. There is a word I have written down on the inside of my hat, with a black marker: *Rinoceronte*. Rhinoceros. It is from a book I like to read for motivation called *El Rinoceronte*. It always helps me, this book. It tells the story of a rhinoceros who tries very hard, in very forceful ways, to be successful. It tells how you have to be fierce and competitive, like a rhinoceros, in everything you do. Whenever I get a new hat, I find a black marker and write down this word on the inside band. It is not because of superstition, but because of tradition. It is a very powerful animal, the rhinoceros, a very powerful word, and so I look at the word to remind myself to be strong. I think about the message of the book and then I put my face in the hat and kiss the word with my lips. I say the word to myself as I do this, for motivation.

It is like a quiet chant, the way I say this word, the way I kiss this word. It is like a silent cry. Always, this is how I begin. I stand behind the pitching mound with my back to home plate. I put my face in my hat and whisper, *"Rinoceronte!"*

And I am ready.

JIM JOYCE

Heading Home

When you've been at this umpiring deal as long as I have, one game runs into another. The airports, the locker rooms . . . even the hotels start to look the same. For us, the base-ball season is one long road trip, broken up by a couple minivacations here and there. We've got a great umpires' union, but it's nothing like the players' union. We're always hopscotching across the country. It's nothing for us to work a series on the east coast to start the week, travel to the west coast for a weekend set, and then hop a plane back to Chicago or Texas to start the next week. Happens all the time.

Wouldn't trade this life for anything, but it takes something out of you. After twenty-plus years, it's a lot of wear and tear and hustle and hassle, but I'm not complaining. Just setting it out there. I've got it better than most because I get to go home every once in a while. Not home to Oregon, where I live with my wife Kay, where we raised our two kids. Nope, home to Ohio, where I grew up. Trips to Detroit or Cleveland, as I said, I stay with my mom at her house in Toledo. Up until last year, it was my dad's house, too, and now I'm back on the anniversary of his passing.

I get in on Sunday evening, and there's a long list of stuff I have to do before the first game of the series on Tuesday. The day off on Monday, Memorial Day, is like a minibreak in the schedule, only it's no vacation. It's not like I'm hanging with the guys on my crew, maybe catching a round of golf or a nice steak dinner. No, there's all sorts of errands I have to run, chores that have piled up around the house. Lightbulbs to change . . . stuff like that. My mom's eighty-six, so she can't really do for herself anymore, so whenever I hit town she has me running around. And I don't mind it, not one bit. I'm not really thinking about this upcoming series, or what these games might mean. I've got to get through my punch list, is all.

The big deal on this trip home is a visit to my dad's grave. First time I've been out to the cemetery since his funeral. First time I'm seeing his headstone—so, yeah, it's a big deal. Huge. I'm all shook up about it, all emotional. Can't think of much else. It's like I'm working through a punch-in-the-stomach list, this trip. And somehow or other, it's all tied in to what I do for a living. One thing about my dad, he got a big kick out of me being an umpire. Never much cared for it himself, but he loved it like crazy that I was doing it. Told all his friends about it. Watched my games whenever he could. Toward the end, he could catch most of them on the Internet. We'd talk three or four times a week and he always had something to say about some call, some play, something. He'd phone me after a controversial call and say, "Man, Jimmy, they were all over so-and-so last night."

And I'd always say, "Never mind that, Dad. One day it can happen to me."

One day, my first full season in the bigs, it did, and I'll tell that story here. Doesn't really go in this part of the book, but I'll tell it anyway, because it's one of those stories I always think about when I think about my dad. Like I said, it's all tied in. He used to love to talk to me about this type of thing, and here I am, in his house, remembering the first time I told him this story. It always got him going, this one. It was July 15, 1989, Angels versus Orioles, Memorial Stadium in Baltimore. Bases loaded, bottom of the ninth, game tied 9–9. The Angels had been up 9–7 to start the inning but the Orioles got a rally going and now Mike Devereaux was up with a runner on first. I was working third base. Devereaux hit a shot down the left-field line, headed for the foul pole. I was in great position to make the call but then, for just a split second, the ball disappeared from view. The only thing I could think was that the ball found a hole in the mesh netting on the fair side of the foul pole. This kind of thing happened from time to time in those old ballparks, and it's the only thing that made sense. I knew the ball was fair, from the way it was traveling, but there was that one sliver of doubt where I couldn't see if the ball went behind the pole or around it. It's the kind of moment you dread as an umpire, because you can only go on gut, and here I'd been at it for only a couple months so my gut wasn't much.

So I thought about it for just a beat and then signaled that the ball was fair, and Devereaux had a walk-off, two-run homer. That's all it was, at first. The Baltimore fans went crazy. Both teams were in first place at the time, so it was an important game. Both teams were looking to get off to a good start in the second half of the season, so while the Orioles were celebrating, the Angels stormed the field in protest. They went crazy, too, only not in a good way. I ended up ejecting five guys that night, including the manager, the pitching coach, and the pitcher. Doesn't happen too often that you eject guys after the game is officially over, but it still sends a message.

I got back into the locker room after the game and I was pretty upset. Remember, it was my first year, and I didn't know what it took to get bounced from this great new job. I thought maybe if I messed up, and if enough people complained, they'd kick me back down to the minors—or maybe all the way out of baseball.

Larry Young was umpiring at second base, and he could see I was stressed. He sat down with me over beers after the game and tried to talk me through it. Said this kind of thing happens all the time. The opposing manager gets all hot, maybe even files a protest, but everything works out fine.

I went back to my hotel room that night and called Kay, told her what had happened. ESPN was still in its infancy back then, but they were showing this call over and over on the highlights. The commentators were raking me over the coals. It was one of the top stories around the league.

Kay said, "So they're upset about the call, but did you get it right?"

I said, "Yeah, I think so, but I'm not a hundred percent sure. I'm pretty sure, just not a hundred percent."

She said, "Well, they keep showing it on television, and they can't tell, either, so pretty sure should be good enough, right?"

I said, "Hope so."

I talked to my dad about it some. He'd seen the play but all he could say was, "If you saw it fair, Jimmy, then it was fair. End of story."

He was my biggest supporter, this was true, but he was also practical.

Next day, I got to the park and they had a closed-circuit television set up in the locker room. They were showing the in-house feed from the day before, and it turned out one of the camera guys had caught the play from just the right angle. They zoomed in and you could clearly see the ball ricochet off the foul pole, which was painted yellow. Of course, if it hits the foul pole, that means it's a fair ball, so I started to feel a whole lot better about my call. And then, just in case I still had any doubts, one of the clubhouse guys pulled the ball from his pocket. The fan who caught it had taken it to the office, thinking it might be something we could use. So I looked at the ball and sure enough there's a yellow scuff mark on it from where it skidded off the pole.

I saw that and thought, *Damn!*

An hour or so later, we were out at home plate, going over the lineups and ground rules, and Doug Rader, the Angels manager, he still wasn't buying it. He was still hot about it, like it had just happened. Now, Doug had been around the game a bunch of years by this point. He was a real character. Played most of his career for the Houston Astros, but he was probably best remembered for his raunchy locker room behavior. There's a famous scene in Jim Bouton's classic baseball book, *Ball Four*, where Rader drops his drawers and squats over a birthday cake and leaves a little extra deposit for the guest of honor. And now he was standing at home plate, still steaming over last night's call, expecting us to take him seriously.

He said, "Okay, which one of you assholes is gonna screw me today?"

Ken Kaiser had the plate that night, so he just flashed Doug Rader one of those *you have got to be kidding me!* looks and ran him from the game. Before the first pitch! (Best I can tell, that makes Doug Rader the only manager run from one game after it ended, and then run from the next game before it even started.) Turned out they were just gearing up for the national anthem on the loudspeaker system, and as Rader was being tossed there was a bunch of yelling and screaming, some of it pretty colorful, but then we all had to stop and take off our hats and show our respect. It's like someone hit a pause button and Rader just froze. We all just froze. And then, soon as we got to the "land of the free" part, we had our hats back on and Rader was jawing at us all over again, calling us "sonsabitches" and a few other things I won't mention here.

Man, my father just loved that story. He thought it was hilarious, that these big leaguers could have these wild temper tantrums, like little kids. We'd talk on and on about this kind of thing, and he'd bust up laughing. And on this Monday afternoon, me running my mom around town, going out to the cemetery and back, getting the house in order, it puts me in mind of how things were between me and my dad. Like I said, the memory doesn't really fit, leading up to this Galarraga game, but at the same time it kinda does. I mean, players have a whole other set of motions they go through as a game approaches. Guys are playing for their jobs, their careers. They're in and out of slumps, scratching for more playing time, battling through injuries. With umpires, it's different. By the time we reach the big league level, this *is* our job. This *is* our career. Oh, we've got performance reviews, more and more these days, but it never happens that an umpire loses his job in the middle of a season over one blown call, one bad game. Basically, we've got nothing left to prove, except that we can get it right each time out. All we can do is all we can do, and then we can check in with our wives and our kids and our parents, first chance we get, and make sure we get it right with them, too.

TWO

ARMANDO GALARRAGA

Tommyjohn

In 1999, there were not enough players for every major league organization to have its own rookie league team in Venezuela, so many teams combined their players. In Spanish, we called the arrangement a *cooperativa*. We played a three-month schedule, in the middle of the summer. Our team, San Joachin, was run by the Montreal Expos, the Los Angeles Dodgers, and the St. Louis Cardinals. We did not play for one or the other. We played for all. For uniforms, we wore yellow jerseys with the Major League Baseball symbol on them, and then we wore a small patch to tell if we belonged to Montreal or Los Angeles or St. Louis. We also wore our own hats, like in an all-star game.

The manager worked for all three major league teams, so he had to find a way to teach three different groups of players from three different organizations, and at the same time he had to win baseball games. It is not such an easy balance, but this man was good for the job. His name was Juan Davalillo.

His brother Vic Davalillo was one of the most famous, most popular players to come from Venezuela. But Juan Davalillo never made it to the big leagues. He was a good player, but there are many good players. However, there are not so many good coaches, and I liked this man very much. He was very patient, very helpful. There was also a pitching coach assigned to this team, who was different than the pitching coach for the Montreal organization. They worked together, but also separately. I was used to only one voice helping me with my pitching and now there were many different voices telling me what to do. It was not so easy to follow everyone's advice, all at the same time. With Henrique, my instructions were only to throw hard and be consistent, but these new coaches had many more things to say, many more things for me to think about. They worked with me on holding runners, on changing the speed of my delivery, on mechanics. Henrique was only teaching what I needed to make a good showing at a tryout. These men were teaching what I needed to win games and to be a professional pitcher. There is a difference.

My very first game as a professional was not so successful. I was pitching in relief against a team of the New York Mets and the Colorado Rockies. I came in at the beginning of the sixth inning, and I was super nervous. I remember I ran in from the outfield, where I had been warming up. It was not really a bullpen, where I had been warming up. It was just a mound on the other side of the outfield fence. I did not run to the infield because I wanted to show the other team that I was confident, or to pump myself up, the way you sometimes see with relief pitchers. No, I ran because I did not know what else to do. I ran because I was excited, and not the good kind of excited. I was the nervous kind of excited. I was so nervous I could not control my pitches. I walked two batters and gave up a base hit. The ball was not hit very hard, but it allowed two runs to score so I came off the field thinking it was a terrible start for my career. I think I even ran off the field to our bench, because I did not think the inning could be over fast enough.

But the pitching coach did not think my performance was so terrible. Or maybe he did and he was trying to be encouraging. He said, "Hey, it is all right. You are still learning."

I was not only learning about pitching that summer. I was also learning about living on my own and managing my expenses. This was a big change from how things were when I was living with my parents in Caracas. We were paid about $300 every two weeks during the rookie league season, and out of that money I had to pay for my food and my room and my other expenses. The $3,500 signing bonus I had given to my parents, but this money was for me to spend and save, however I needed, however I wished. My parents helped me to get organized and find a place to live, but after that I was on my own. It was a lot of responsibility. My friends back home in Caracas did not have such responsibility. They only had to go to school, get good grades, and keep out of trouble, but this was a job. It was baseball, and it was my dream, but it was also a job.

The philosophy of the rookie league was for us to progress as players. We were trying to win, but we were also trying to improve. It was the same balance for the manager, but for us it was also a personal matter. It was making sure we were growing as players. This was even more important than winning. I did not understand this in the moment, when I was pitching, but this was so. The coaches did not care how many zeroes I put up as a pitcher. They only cared that I improved, that I was learning. And that I was getting stronger. In the beginning, I was throwing eighty-four, eighty-five on the radar gun, and I finished the summer throwing eighty-nine. I was only seventeen years old, so this was very good velocity for someone so young.

The true goal for each of us on that team was to get a visa. This was not discussed in just this way, but this was the reality. This meant that the goal was not only to improve, but to improve in a more promising way than our Montreal teammates. We could only be promoted if there were enough visas, because in Venezuela there was only this one rookie league and the local academies, so we were competing with each other for very few spots. Also, if you did not get your visa after three seasons, you would get released, so there was an additional pressure on each player to do well right away. You can see, it was possible to play well and be deserving of promotion, but if another, less-deserving player was completing his third season he might get the visa instead. It would come down to what was best for the organization. It would not always be what was best for you.

There were too many things to worry about, too many things I could not control, so I only cared that I improved. That was my focus. I finished the summer in a positive way but I did not get a visa, so I could not go to the United States. A part of me could understand this. Today, major league teams have many more visas to distribute to their young players, but in 1999 this was not the case. For the Montreal Expos group assigned to San Joachin there were only four visas, so they went to some of the older, more established players, and to one or two who were in danger of being released.

I went back to Caracas believing I would use the off-season to work on my conditioning and my training. I threw every day. Some people did not agree with this idea. My mother, for example, thought I should continue with my education or perhaps find some type of regular job. I also had a girlfriend at the time, and her mother was not too happy that I was a baseball player, so I had to be nice and respectful and listen to her advice about what I should do. I did not always want to hear this advice from my girlfriend's mother. She used to sit me down on her couch and say, "What happens if you break your arm, Armando? What are you going to do then?"

My plan was to play for a team in the Venezuelan league, the *Liga Venezolana de Béisbol Profesional*. This was a very exciting prospect for me, because as a boy this was the very highest level of baseball in Venezuela. The games were on television. The stadiums were filled with many thousands of people. A lot of famous major league players came to play there—not only Venezuelan players but players from the United States and from all over the world. The season was from October to January. Montreal had an arrangement with a team called *Tiburones de la Guaira,* and they wanted me to pitch for them so they could follow my progress, but I wanted to play for *Leones del Caracas*. This was the team I always rooted for as a small boy. I did not wish to be difficult, or to go against the people from Montreal, but I did not wish to pass up a chance to play for my favorite team, so I asked if I could try out for *Leones*, just to see what would happen. If I did not make it, I would play for *Tiburones*.

Happily, the people from *Leones* wanted me to pitch for them, and the people from Montreal decided to allow it. They did not have to allow it, but they were being considerate. Everyone was in agreement. I did not make the main team, however. If I am being honest, this was what I expected. In Venezuela, the professional league is set up with a big team and a little team. It is like how in the United States there is a major league team and a minor league team, only in Venezuela there is just one minor league team. The scouts from the little team liked how I pitched and thought I could be a starter. One of them said to me, "You are tall, your ball moves well, you can win some games for us."

And I did. I had a very good season playing for the little *Leones* team, winning seven games with an earned run average under 3.00. These were very good numbers for someone so young, very encouraging. In fact, the *Leones* coaches were so impressed with my pitching they invited me to join the big team when we finished our season. It is like the September call-ups in the major leagues, when the minor league teams have finished their season, and here it meant I could play with some of my very favorite players, like Bobby Abreu and Henry Blanco. Magglio Ordonez was in the league that year, on a different team. It was a great big honor, and a great big difference from my time with the little team. For those games, we had only thirty or forty people in the stands. For these games with the big team, the stadium was filled with over forty thousand people, so it was like going from a low minor league team all the way to Yankee Stadium.

I can still remember how proud my father was when I told him I was going to play for the big team. His pride was even bigger than the day I signed my professional contract, because *Leones* was his team, too. We all cheered for *Leones* in our family. I only pitched in relief, and only in one or two games, but it was a very exciting time. It was a time for dreaming.

The next year, I was not so successful. The people from Montreal had been following my progress with the little *Leones* team. They saw my numbers, and spoke to my coaches, so when I returned to the San Joachin rookie league team for my second season in the summer of 2000 there were a lot of expectations. Most of these I placed on myself, because I wanted very much to be offered a visa at the end of the season. The trouble with this plan was that I did not have such good control of my curveball. The coaches had seen that I had pitched as a starter for the little *Leones* team so they decided to make me a starter. That would be my future, everyone agreed, and when you are a starter you must be able to throw many different pitches. Already I had a good fastball and a good changeup. My slider and my curveball could be very good, very effective, but sometimes I struggled with them, and that is how it was as this new season began. In my first few starts I pitched very well. Then I became wild with my pitches. I walked a lot of hitters. My curveball had a big, big break, but I could not always make it break the way I wanted. I could not always keep it in the strike zone, so my earned run average went up, up, up. My pitching coach tried to work with me to fix the problem, but every time he told me to change my release point, so it wasn't so high, I kept hearing my father's voice telling me to throw from the highest possible position, to throw down, down, down. It was the opposite advice, and I did not know how to balance one against the other.

I kept wishing I could switch my numbers from the little *Leones* team to the San Joachin rookie league team because, of course, the Montreal Expos did not have anything to do with the *Leones*. They cared only what I was showing them on their rookie league team, so once again I did not get a visa. This time I was even more disappointed because I had only one more season to prove myself or I would be released. In just two seasons I went from being seventeen years old and feeling no pressure to looking ahead to my next season at nineteen and feeling a lot of pressure.

After the season, I went home to relax for about a month, but before joining the little *Leones* team for a second season I was invited to Montreal's academy in Caracas to work out in front of a few of their scouts. For the first time since I signed with Montreal, I did not touch a baseball for many, many weeks. And now the people at the academy wanted to see how I was doing, how I was progressing, so they put me in a bullpen and asked me to throw. I was not so very nervous this time, because I did not think there was anything to be nervous about. I was just going to throw a few pitches so the scouts could see my progress, so that is what I did. All of a sudden, I was throwing ninety-two, ninety-three, which was a big jump for me. I think there was even one pitch at ninety-four miles per hour, which was superfast for me. The scouts, they could not believe it, because I did not have the reputation for someone who threw with such velocity, so the people at the academy became very excited. I was excited, too, but I did not want to show it. A part of me did not trust that the radar gun was accurate, because I had never thrown so hard in my life.

Someone suggested they find a hitter to put in the batter's box. Very quickly, the scouts arranged for a few batters to stand in against me, and all they could do was swing and swing. Whatever I threw, they kept missing, and each time they missed I felt more relaxed, more confident. My arm was loose. People were coming out to the field to see me throw, because this was not what anyone was expecting.

After my session, we talked about what was different about how I was pitching and the scouts seemed to think that my arm was now rested for the first time in a long while. This made sense. All along, my arm had not been prepared for so much pitching. I was still growing, still developing, and I had not given myself any time to allow my body to recover. I had gone from my first rookie league season to pitching all those innings for the little *Leones* team, to pitching in relief in some late-season games for the big *Leones* team, and then right back for another rookie league season, this time as a starter struggling with my control. It is possible I was too young for so much pitching. My arm was tired, and now that I had rested it for a month it was feeling stronger.

This was a good and welcome thing, because I had been feeling very unhappy about my performance in my second rookie league season. The Montreal scouts, too, were also probably worried that I had not developed so much as a pitcher. But now I was strong and pitching well and everyone became very excited.

At the end of the session, one of the Montreal scouts looked at me and said, "Maybe we should take this guy."

He asked Fred Ferrera, the guy who signed me, what he thought about this.

Fred Ferrera had always been one of my biggest supporters. He said, "Armando has great promise. He will show you something."

The Montreal scouts had already told the four rookie league players about their visas, and they did not have another visa to give to me, so my good news meant one of these players would have to be disappointed. That is the way of things in baseball. There are a limited number of spots, so for every player going up there is another player going down, and I could not let myself worry about that. I could not let someone else's disappointment get in the way of my own happiness. I told myself that this player was going to be released anyway. If not now, then soon. And if it was not me going to take his place, it would be someone else. In my head, this was how I could apologize for what was happening. It did not need an apology, but I felt bad about it. I felt good and bad, all at the same time.

In baseball, there is what you expect and what you cannot expect, and after that there is what you cannot even imagine. Here is what I mean: for two years of rookie ball in Venezuela, I was hoping to pitch well enough to get a visa. That was my only goal. Finally, I made it. But then something happened that almost ended my career, almost before it started.

I went back to pitch winter ball for the little *Leones* team, only now the Expos took more of an involvement in my off-season activity. They instructed the Caracas team to keep me on a pitch count because they liked that my arm was so strong. I was still a starting pitcher, but I did not start so often. In Venezuela, in the minor league, it is not like it is in the United States. You do not have a five-man rotation. There are many pitchers, working on many different things, on many different schedules. Some pitchers take their regular turn and others pitch once a week and others pitch once in a while. I pitched well every time I was given the ball, and then I rested after the season for another few weeks before going to Montreal's main rookie league, in Jupiter, Florida.

I had been to the United States only once before, on a vacation to Disney World with my family. This time I came by myself. It was exciting, like Disney World, only in a different way. The major league players were already in Canada to start the season. When they left Jupiter, the minor league players were just arriving. Triple A, Double A, High A, Middle A, rookie ball . . . we were all going to minor league spring training where the major league Expos had just finished their spring training. It was very special, to be playing on the same fields and changing in the same lockers as these great players. It was like being in school back in Caracas, where we all shared the same building. First the little kids would go in the morning, then the older kids would go in the afternoon. We could close our eyes and imagine we were the same.

Jupiter was a nice place, but I did not know anyone. My English was not very good, and on top of that I was very shy. I do not know if I was shy because my English was not very good, or if one thing had nothing to do with the other. I ate most of my meals at Subway, because I could stand behind the counter and point to whatever I wanted. I did not have to learn the words for tomatoes or onions or ketchup or mustard. I could just point and the person making the sandwich would know what I wanted.

There was an English class for the Latin players, arranged by the Expos. They had many different classes, many different programs to help us feel comfortable, but it was hard for me to feel comfortable. We were far from home, and working very hard to get noticed on the field, trying to make an impression. I was a little bit homesick. I missed my girlfriend. I missed my friends. I missed my family.

My time on the field was a little easier than my time off the field. When I was playing, there was no time to worry about anything but baseball. I did not win a lot of games, but I had a good earned run average and I threw a lot of pitches. My velocity was about ninety-two, ninety-three. This was very good for me, for someone so young, but my curveball was still wild. Some days it would go from side to side. Some days, up and down. Some days I could throw it for strikes. It was hard to guess what it would do.

The money was not so much better in American rookie ball than it was in Venezuela. I was making about $350 every two weeks, but the Expos paid for my food. They gave us tickets, which we could use in some of the restaurants around town, like Subway and Denny's, which I also liked because there were pictures on the menus and I could point there, too.

The Expos also paid for my room in a hotel, which I shared with another player from Venezuela. His name was Salomon Manrique. We got along well, but his English was no better than mine. Together, we did not know very much, but this was not such a big problem because we were so busy with baseball. We went to the stadium every morning at seven o'clock, and we did not get back until seven o'clock at night. It was a long, long day, and when we had an away game it was even longer. Usually our games were at twelve or one o'clock, and after the game we would have lunch in the clubhouse. Then there was a meeting about the game, and then special meetings with our special coaches. After that, we took our showers and received our treatments, and then we were driven back to our hotel. As soon as we got back to the hotel, most of us would go to sleep right away because we were so tired.

It was a very lonely, very difficult time. Most of us did not have cell phones or computers, so it was also very boring. There was not a lot to do when we were not playing. For away games, it was even more difficult, because sometimes we would drive many miles. Sometimes we would go to Vero Beach or Melbourne, so we would leave very early and come back very late. I remember feeling tired, always tired. On the field, my arm was alive and strong and I was putting up good numbers, so it helped to think about this whenever I was feeling lonely or tired in my room.

I saved most of my money that first year, but I did buy a lot of shoes. This was my one vice. I did not know this word, *vice,* when I came to Jupiter, but one of my teammates taught it to me to describe how I was about shopping for shoes. It was like a bad habit. For some reason, I found out in Florida that I really liked shoes, so I used to go to a store called Ross and shop. My closet filled up with shoes. It was a very big store, and I would walk up and down the aisles and feel like I was in an amusement park. I did the same thing in Wal-Mart and Target. There were so many things to see, so many things to try. Before I went back to Venezuela, I bought some new T-shirts, some new boxers, some socks, and many, many pairs of shoes. I looked really nice. I was a professional baseball player in the United States, and when I went home to Caracas I wanted to make a good impression.

At home, things were starting to be a little different. My friends were now finished with high school and many of them were starting university. Everybody had grown up since the time I first went to Valencia to play for San Joachin. Everybody was in a new direction. But I was still the only one who had lived in the United States, so they all wanted to know about American women, American food, American nightclubs, and I did not really know about such things.

I signed again to play that winter with *Leones,* and I thought this time I might be able to make the big team. I was still kind of a rookie, but I had been called up to the big *Leones* team at the end of my first season, and now I had been pitching in the United States, so I thought my chances were good. But I did not make it. The other pitchers, they were probably better. They had more experience. I was disappointed but I told myself it would be for the best. For this season, I was not on such a strict pitch count. The Expos were not worried so much about my innings, so I pitched and pitched. I think now, looking back, that this was a mistake, to pitch so much during the season and then to keep pitching all winter, but I did not say anything. I did not even think about this. I was only happy that they wanted me to pitch.

The reason I now think this was a mistake was because the next season, 2002, was disappointing. The first disappointment was that I was sent once again to the rookie league. In baseball, it is a lot like high school and college. You want to keep moving up, to get to the next level. If you do not move up, from rookie ball to Middle A, from High A to Double A, it means you are not progressing. It means your career is not going anywhere. If you spend too much time not moving up, you will be released. And so there is always a pressure to keep moving forward. As soon as you get to spring training, they tell you where you are. At the Expos stadium in Jupiter, there was a big wall where they put up all the rosters for all of the different levels. They go up on the wall at the same time, and everybody is looking for their name, to see where they have been assigned. I looked and looked for my name, together with a big crowd of players looking for their names. Finally, I found it: I was on the list for the Middle A team in Clinton, Illinois, and I thought this was a good sign. I was moving in the right direction. I was happy.

But then as soon as spring training started I was not feeling so good about my chances of ever making it to Clinton. I could not get anybody out when I was pitching. I could not throw strikes. I did not have the same velocity, the same command. The radar gun was down to eighty-three, eighty-one, which was a big drop. My arm was sore. I could not understand it. The coaches would ask me if there was anything wrong, and my English was only good enough for me to tell them I was sore. I could rub my shoulder and my elbow, to show them where. The people from Montreal, they were worried about this. They took an MRI, to see if this would explain the problem, but the pictures did not show that anything was wrong. The doctor could not tell us the problem. So I kept pitching. They gave me ice, thinking it would help. They gave me heat, thinking it would help. And always they would send me to the mound to pitch.

At the end of spring training I was not on any of the rosters. I did not make any team, at any level, so I went back to Jupiter for another season of rookie ball. It was like a demotion, but I could not pitch because my arm was too sore. They made me get a second MRI, but it also did not show anything. The doctor said my ligaments looked fine, my tendons looked fine. Everything, fine. There was even a third MRI, and after these pictures came back I could hear some of the coaches and the other players whispering that the problem with my arm was in my head. In English, I knew the word "pussy," which was what they were starting to call me. At first, they called me this behind my back, where I could not see, but then some of the coaches started saying it right in front of me. One day, my pitching coach challenged me. His name was Mark Grater. He said, "Are you sure you really want to be here, Armando?"

He was trying to motivate me, I believe, but he did not do such a good job of it.

The Expos had the idea that I should not throw so hard, that maybe this was the problem, so I tried this a few times but my arm was still hurting. At last I stopped pitching. In June, July, August, I did not touch a baseball. I lost the whole season trying to pitch, trying to understand what was wrong with my arm, why it was not working.

At the end of the 2002 season, the Expos sent me for a fourth MRI. For this one, they injected a special color in my arm, a red dye, to help them see better in the pictures. The doctor explained what he was doing and it felt to me like I was in a science fiction movie. I was certain that Montreal was going to release me. I was costing them so much money, with all of these tests, and I was not making progress. I was moving in the wrong direction.

Finally, the pictures from the MRI showed that something was wrong. The doctor came to discuss it with me and one of my coaches. He explained that the ligaments in my arm were torn and that I would need surgery. "He should not be pitching," he said. "It is no wonder."

This was a great relief, but it was also a worry. I did not have to prove any more that I was truly hurt, but now I had to worry if they could fix my injury. The doctor explained that I needed Tommy John surgery. I had never heard this name. I did not know it was the name of a pitcher who was the first person to have this type of surgery. I heard it as "Tommyjohn," like one long word, yet another phrase I did not understand:

"Oh, Armando, he need Tommyjohn." They kept saying it, over and over, fast, fast, fast.

Tommyjohn, Tommyjohn, Tommyjohn.

I was relieved that the doctors could finally explain why my arm had been so sore, but I was also frustrated. In English, I heard my teammates use the word "pissed," and this explained how I felt. I was not really mad but I was pissed, which was a special kind of mad. For the whole season nobody believed that I was hurt, and now they said I needed an operation to fix the ligaments in my arm. I went from where nothing was wrong to where everything was wrong. The doctors and coaches said it was because of pitching too much, too soon. Summer league, rookie league, winter league . . . all year long, I was pitching, pitching, pitching, but my arm was not strong enough for so much work. My arm was not so mature.

The Expos sent me to Birmingham, Alabama, to see a doctor named Dr. James Andrews. They said he was the expert for *Tommyjohns*, which someone finally explained to me was the name of a pitcher, Tommy John. Dr. Andrews examined me and looked at the pictures and agreed with the doctor from Jupiter, so they did the operation. It is a very complicated operation. They had to take a tendon from my knee and put it in my arm. Usually they take a tendon from your opposite arm, but for me they decided to take from my knee. I was scared about this when they explained it to me. I was all by myself. Nobody from the Expos came to help me. Nobody from home. There was just me.

For two or three weeks, I was in a hotel room close to the hospital. I could not even get out of bed while I was recovering from the surgery because of my knee. I was calling my friends and my family on the telephone, crying, but they could not help me from so far away. They could only tell me to calm down, but it is easy to *tell* someone to calm down. It is not so easy to calm down.

Whenever somebody from the Expos called I said I wanted to go home. I complained that nobody in Birmingham could speak Spanish, so they agreed to send me to Jupiter for rehabilitation. In Florida, at least, there would be people from the Expos to check on me, people who spoke Spanish. I would not be so all alone.

There were a few other players doing rehabilitation in Jupiter, so I felt a little better there. They put me in a room with an American player and we helped each other. We would go to our rehab sessions together and give each other strength and motivation.

The first thing to feel better was my knee, which was how the doctor said it would happen. After about six weeks, I could walk on it without feeling any pain, so in my rehab I kept working on my knee to make it stronger and stronger. It meant I could move around without having to ask for help. It also meant I could start to focus on my arm, which was still very tender. This worried me, that my arm was not recovering the same as my knee. I did not feel any strength in my arm. I did not think I could throw a baseball ever again, but I did not tell anybody about this worry because I did not want anyone from the Expos to have doubts about me and my pitching.

The whole time I was in Birmingham, and then in Jupiter, I was not getting paid. This was not such a big concern because the Expos were covering my expenses, but I was not earning a salary so I did not feel like I needed to stay in Florida. It was very depressing. Even with the other players for company and motivation, it was very lonely. Every day, I would go to rehab at seven o'clock in the morning and by nine or ten o'clock I would be back in my room with nothing to do. All day long there was nothing to do, so I wanted to go home to Venezuela. In Venezuela, at least, I could do nothing with my friends and my family. I could be more comfortable. Once again, I started to complain to the people from the Expos. They wanted me to finish my rehab in Jupiter so they could follow my progress, but I complained so much they finally agreed to send me home in November. I had to promise not to throw a baseball and to continue with my exercises, and I was happy to make these promises. It was for me that I would do these things, not only for the Expos.

The physical therapist also gave me new exercises to add to my rehab as my arm started to feel stronger. My parents helped me with these exercises. At home, they were my physical therapists. Every day, we would do the rice exercise. My mom would fill a bucket with rice, and I would put my hand inside and do my exercises. This is very common for people recovering from Tommy John. The rice is soft and smooth but it gives you some tension so you can work your tendons and fingers. *Resistance,* that is the word for what the rice provides, and it gives you only a small amount of resistance, so you can feel like you are making progress.

I was surprised that something so simple could work so well, but soon I started to think it would not be so long before

I could throw a baseball. All that winter, I did not throw. I worked out with weights and ran, and I got myself in good shape for baseball, all the time never touching a baseball. Finally, when it was time for spring training, I went back to Jupiter. I did not like how my arm felt the first time I tried to throw. It felt puffy and weak. I did not recognize this feeling. The Expos did not like it either. They did not like it so much that they did not put me on a roster at the end of spring training. For the third year in a row, I stayed in Jupiter for extended spring training, for rookie ball. It was another big disappointment. But the Expos, they did not seem so disappointed. They told me not to worry so much about my pitching that year, to worry only about getting stronger, about recovering from the Tommy John. Most pitchers, when they have Tommy John, they have a full year of recovery. It takes a long time for the ligament from one part of your body to adjust to being in a different part of your body, for the ligament to get strong. This was how the doctor had explained my recovery, but I did not think the normal rules would be for me. I thought because I was young and strong I would recover faster than normal. I thought I would be ready for the season, but I was not ready.

I was not even ready for the winter season with the little *Leones* team. The Expos wanted me to pitch in the Venezuelan league, to get strong for the 2004 season. Already I had missed almost two full seasons with this injury, and they did not want me to miss a third, but as soon as I started pitching for *Leones* I could see that my arm was not right. The pitching coach examined my delivery and told me I should stop throwing a curveball. He thought this might be the reason

I was having trouble with my recovery. He even thought it might have been the cause of my trouble in the first place, because the way I threw the curveball, there was a very big snap of my wrist, which caused a lot of tension in my arm. With my slider, there was not such a big snap so there was not so much tension.

I listened to this advice because it made sense, and soon my arm began to feel better. My velocity began to return. I did not mind so much, not throwing my curveball. For many years, I could not get my curveball to do what I wanted it to do, so I was happy to be done with it. And now that my arm was getting stronger, I did not miss that pitch. My slider was good, with a nice break, and I was able to throw it with good control, so this helped to make my fastball and my changeup more effective. Everything was going good, so I was placed on the roster for the Middle A team, in Savannah, Georgia. The pitching coach there was Ricky Bones. He was a very good major league pitcher from Puerto Rico, and he liked the way I was throwing, so he made me a part of his rotation. I ended up having a very good year in Savannah. My numbers were good.

Savannah was also good for a personal reason because I met my wife that season. Christin. She is from Chicago, but we met in Georgia, where she was working for the Expos as a strength and conditioning coach. She was one of my rehab trainers, so this was another very positive benefit to the season. She could speak only a little bit of Spanish and I could speak only a little bit of English, but we could meet in the middle and help each other.

In 2005, I started playing High A ball in Potomac, Virginia, where I was named to the all-star team for the Carolina League. Later that season, I went to Double A, in Harrisburg, Pennsylvania, and at the end of the year it said in *Baseball America* that I was one of the top pitching prospects in the organization. This was a very important moment for my career. It also said that I almost made it to the major leagues that year, as a September call-up for the Washington Nationals, which was the new name of the Montreal Expos. But I did not finish strong that season. I pitched over 150 innings, which was more than I had ever pitched, so my arm was a little tired.

I did not mind so much that I was not a September call-up. Why? I cannot be certain, but for so many years I had been dreaming of playing for the Expos. Ever since they signed me and I put on my Montreal hat, this had been my goal. When I was recovering from my surgery, all I could think was how important it was to make it to Montreal. But now, very quickly, the team had moved to Washington, DC, and I did not feel the same connection. Yes, the most important thing was to make it to the major leagues, but I did not feel so disappointed when I did not get called to join the Nationals that year. Maybe if the team was still playing in Canada I would have felt differently. Who can say?

But that is how it is in baseball. There is what you expect and what you cannot expect, and then there is what you cannot even imagine. Soon I would find this out all over again.

JIM JOYCE

Fly-Away Arms

Umpires have their little idiosyncrasies. They punch a guy out on strikes, they thrust out their right arm with a flourish and bark out a call that doesn't sound like any call in nature. Or maybe they step emphatically toward first, or do a kind of fist pump in the air. Some guys work fast. Some guys are more patient, like they're taking time to think things through. And then there are some guys who are so subtle you can hardly tell if a pitch is a strike or a ball, or if a runner is safe or out.

Guess you could say it takes all kinds in umpiring, just like in anything else. Everybody puts their own stamp on the job but the thing of it is, with umpires, we seem to come by our stamps naturally. They reflect our personalities. It's not like there are too many kids out there dreaming of growing up to become major league umpires, practicing their calls in front of a mirror the way other kids might practice their batting stances or pitching motions. It's not like you come up with some signature move and hope it gets you noticed so you can land a job out of Bradenton.

In fact, it's just the opposite. The first couple weeks at umpire school, everybody was identical. We moved around on the field like robots. There might have been some tiny differences in our strike zones but our calls were exactly the same. Balls, strikes, outs . . . you couldn't tell one of us from the other. Our positioning, our approach . . . exactly the same, all the way down to the tone of our voice. It's not like we were afraid to be different, to be ourselves, to stand out. It's just that we were clearly told this was the way it was. We were instructed to do things a certain way. They used to tell us to stand in front of a mirror and practice the standard safe call, the standard out call. And a lot of guys did just that, which made for some pretty funny scenes each night in the common shower house we all shared.

Our instructors wanted everything done by the book, and if we varied our calls in any way we got a talking to. Looking back, I think the idea was that we couldn't be ourselves until we could be like everyone else. It wasn't until the fifth and final week of the program, when they sent us out to start calling actual games, that we were encouraged to develop our own styles on the field. When I got to Bradenton, though, I was still a little timid, still in my robotic umpiring mode. At Bradenton, I remember making a safe call at first base that got the attention of my instructor, only not in a good way. He came up to me after the game and said, "Jimmy, you've got fly-away arms."

I had no idea what he was talking about. *Fly-away arms?* I'd never heard the expression. I didn't know fly-away arms from regular arms. Turned out he meant that I was bringing my arms up way too high and that they needed to be a little flatter. I was flapping them up and back, almost like a swimmer getting ready to dive into a pool before a race.

The instructor dropped his clipboard and demonstrated. He said, "Cup your hands so they cut through the wind better."

That always stuck with me, the bit about cupping my hands, and for a long time I kept it in mind whenever I threw my arms out to call a guy safe. Even practiced it for a while, I'll admit. I don't think of it any more, and I sure as heck don't practice it, but by this point I have it down. By this point, I'm not flying away.

Very quickly, I realized my voice stood out as an umpire. I was only trying to be heard, but it came out sounding pretty emphatic. To this day, I'm known for my loud calls. It's my most distinctive quality on the field. When I call somebody "Out!" or "Safe!" he damn sure knows it. Everybody knows it. When I'm working the plate, same thing. If it catches the inside corner, I'll let you know. Right away. Last thing you want, as an umpire, is for the players not to hear the call. With me, there's no room for doubt.

Sometimes the student umpires would get together and compare notes. Guys would ask each other about this or that gesture, this or that call. They'd borrow from what they liked and find a way to make it their own. But this didn't happen as much as you'd think. Typically, it was the middle tier of umpires studying this kind of thing so closely. The guys at the bottom couldn't be bothered, and the guys at the top didn't see the need. It was the middle group that kept looking over each other's shoulders, trying to find some kind of edge. I counted myself among the top group, so I just did my own thing. If one of the instructors pointed something out to me, I'd be sure to listen, maybe even make some changes if I thought it might help, but other than that I tried to go at it with my own flair, my own personality. Told myself I'd either make it on my own or fall flat.

In Sarasota, I was assigned to a crew with an umpire from Triple A and an umpire from Double A, and then there was me and one other newbie looking to latch on. Our Triple A ump, Tom Lepperd, acted as crew chief. I hadn't been hired yet, so I had to assume there was a supervisor at every game, tracking my every move, although in practical terms I knew this wasn't the case. There weren't enough supervisors to go around, but I told myself early on to do my job as if I were being watched all the time. To this day, that's been my approach.

With about ten days to go in spring training, Tom Lepperd got a call telling him his crew's assignments. He already knew he was working the American Association that season. Our Double A ump was being sent to the Eastern League. And then there was me and the other newbie, a Wendelstedt guy named Paul Bonnicksen, and we were hoping for any assignment at all. Most likely we'd be headed to some rookie league, which was known as Short A because they played a much shorter season, starting in June. That's where most of us straight out of umpire school were headed. That is, if we weren't headed home. Not everybody got the call.

The day our assignments were handed out, Tom Lepperd came over to me and said, "You must have done something right. They're sending you to the Midwest League."

At that time, teams in the Midwest played what was known as Long A ball. It was a full season, starting in April, and a notch above a Short A assignment. I was thrilled, because it meant someone liked me enough to skip me past the first level, but also because it meant more work, more money. We would play in towns like Cedar Rapids, Iowa, and Wausau, Wisconsin. All along the blue highways of the Midwest. I pulled out a map, to get a sense of where I'd be the rest of the summer, and the good news was that one town wasn't too far from another. With any luck, I'd tiptoe around the league without too many long-haul trips.

I had about a week before I was due to report to league headquarters in Burlington, Iowa, so I gathered my things and drove back home to Toledo for a couple days. Filled my parents in on what was going on, what this new assignment meant. They were happy for me, because I was happy, but underneath they weren't thrilled. My father kept asking, "You sure you want to do this, Jimmy?" He couldn't understand why I'd walk away from all that money at Jeep, why I wanted to drive along those back roads, why I wasn't using my education. He was an athlete and a big-time baseball fan, so he understood the pull of the game, but he didn't understand . . . this.

He had a point, I'll admit. It can be a hard life, an umpiring life. But when you sign on to it and it gets in your blood it's hard to think of doing anything else.

* * *

Umpiring is like anything else. There's a progression to it, same way there is for players. You want to keep moving through the ranks, from the low minors all the way up through Triple A and on to the bigs. Most of all, you don't want to be stuck in the same place for any great stretch of time. If you are, it usually means someone is trying to tell you something.

There's a whole culture to it, too. You pick it up as you go along. Right away, I got that your first year is key. The goal is to at least make it back to that same level the following year. If you can get out of that first year and move up to the next level, you're on your way. If you're simply invited back to where you are, that's okay, but if you get sent down a notch you're basically done. Again, someone is trying to tell you something.

Second year, there are a whole new set of goals. Here you want to get promoted at some point during the season. People don't realize it, but there's a whole lot of movement in umpiring, up and down, same way there is with players. One guy gets hurt or moved up, someone is brought in to fill his spot. There's a domino effect, all across baseball. You start to know how many umpiring jobs there are at each level. You know who's retiring, who's struggling, who's sick, who's injured . . . whatever. It's a small community, the professional umpiring community, so everybody knows everybody. Your ups and downs and comings and goings are tracked by your peers.

Can't say for sure if this is a good thing or a bad thing, but it's definitely a thing. Definitely something to think about. When you're out there, banging around those small Midwestern towns, killing time between games, there's not a whole lot to do but sit and talk to your fellow umpires. In A ball, that meant just one fellow umpire—my first partner, Jim Johnston. You end up talking a lot of baseball, a lot of situations. Jim was a little older than me, so he was kind of like a big brother. Plus, he'd already worked a year of rookie ball, so he had me on experience, too. He knew the drill. He knew what restaurants to go to, what bars to go to, where to stay. Remember, this was before cell phones and computers, so there was a sort of umpiring network, and Jim knew how to tap in to it. We spent a lot of time in telephone booths, as I recall. In fact, I used to charge all my long distance calls to my parents, and they weren't too happy about it. They kept a running tab. Whenever I called home, they said, "Jimmy, you're up to twenty bucks for long distance calls."

I almost quit midway through my first season. It was just a hiccup—the one and only time I second-guessed what I was doing. And it's not like there was anything else I wanted to do more. What happened was, the first Fourth of July weekend on the road, I woke up feeling homesick. Surprised the heck out of me that I'd get to feeling this way, because I'd been having the time of my life, but then I thought about it and it made sense. You see, my mom and dad always threw a great big Fourth of July party back home. I'd been a part of those celebrations for as long as I could remember. Hadn't missed one, even during college. And here I woke up feeling like I was missing out, knowing Jim and I were looking at another long drive, knowing we'd have to scramble to find a place to stay and a plate of something decent to eat, knowing I was looking ahead to another couple months of more of the same. And so for that one day I just felt like packing it in.

You know how you hear people say there was a point in their careers when they felt like they'd finally made it, like they had arrived? Well, with me it was just the opposite. I woke up that morning and saw the path I was on, and it felt like it wasn't taking me anywhere I was meant to go. All I could see was that it was taking me away from my friends and family. All I could see was a long, hard road. So I thought about quitting, just then. Even calculated how long it would take me to drive home after the game, from Burlington, Iowa, to Toledo, to see if I could make it in time for my parents' party.

Told myself I'd work the game that afternoon and then break the news to Jim, but on the way to the ballpark the feeling started to pass. Wasn't quite an epiphany, but it felt like a return to my senses. Ended up picking things up a notch out on the field that afternoon. Jim had the plate, so I was on the bases, and I remember feeling like I was kind of floating out there on the field. I was moving well, had great positioning, was really feeling on my game. By the time the game was over, I couldn't even remember why I'd been so down about things.

I told Jim about it afterward. I said, "I was gonna quit today."

He said, "Why didn't you say something?"

I said, "I'm saying something now."

He said, "No, I mean earlier."

And all I could say was, "I don't know. Wasn't sure about it, I guess. Just woke up this morning feeling a little homesick, was all it was."

And so we moved on to our next town, our next series, our next stretch of more of the same, and I never once regretted it.

Wasn't a whole lot of money coming my way that first year so we tried to keep a lid on our expenses. Jim and I shared a room. We shared car expenses and got by on cheap eats. We were run pretty ragged, driving from town to town, staying in roadside motels. One thing: it's tough to take care of yourself under those conditions, and I did such a lousy job of it I came down with mono. Didn't even make it to the play-offs that first year. The last week of the season, I had to fly home to Toledo and leave Jim to work the rest of the schedule on his own. They brought in a local guy to fill in, but Jim had to work the plate for seven days in a row. We still talk about that, me leaving him stranded at the butt end of the season.

Left him with my car, though. There was no other way for him to get to the last couple series, so he needed it more than I did. The understanding was he'd drive it back to Toledo from his last game, which was in Cedar Rapids, Iowa, that year. Then he'd visit for a day or two and fly back to Mitchell, South Dakota, where he'd spend the off-season working in his dad's sporting goods store.

My first off-season wasn't much. Took a while for me to fully recover from the mono, but I was back on my feet in time for the school and Catholic Youth Organization basketball seasons. I could make ten dollars a game, refereeing, so I'd try to set it up so that I had four or five games on Saturdays and Sundays. Midweek, I could only squeeze in one or two, afternoons and evenings. I also did a lot of substitute teaching. Hadn't really saved any money while I was on the road in the Midwest League, so I grabbed what I could. Every now and then, one of my parents would push me to think about hiring on at Jeep, but I couldn't bring myself to do it. It's not that I minded the hard work, or the grind, but I guess I was worried I'd get sucked in by the good pay, the benefits, the job security . . . everything I didn't have as a minor league umpire.

All I had as an ump was the smell of the game. And I'll tell you what: it was plenty. Folks don't believe me when I explain how things were, starting out, but I was perfectly content. Other than that one hiccup, it was one big kick. It was a treading water kind of existence, though, and I couldn't save any money. During the season, my ten-dollar per diem didn't even cover my expenses, so I had to dip into my salary, which was just about five hundred bucks a month. And out of that I had to buy my own gear. Lucky for me, Jim could get us some deals through his dad's store, but it still ran into money. I had to buy my own pants, my own shirts, my own shoes. For a while I got by wearing a hand-me-down face mask from my buddy Larry Owen, and a catcher's chest protector, but these didn't really cut it behind the plate, so I had to replace them before long. When we graduated from umpire school, they gave us a brochure for a special store that carried all kinds of umpiring gear—chest protectors, shin guards, what have you—and I ended up spending about $150 before I'd even drawn my first paycheck, so I started out feeling so far behind it was like I'd never get ahead.

Oh, man, I wore some of that gear into the ground, but I had to replace the first pair of ump shoes I ever bought. I thought I could save some money with a pair that doubled as base shoes and plate shoes. Most plate shoes have metal toes and a special flap that goes over the top of your foot to keep foul balls from breaking all those bones. You were supposed to wear a different kind in the field, because the plate shoes tended to be a little heavy and you didn't need all that protection out there, but I found this one company that made a pair of base shoes with an extra piece you could Velcro on when you were working the plate. It was a pretty clever design, but it didn't work so great. I took my first foul ball off my foot and right away got to thinking I should have spent the extra money on the other shoes.

By the end of my first season my bank account looked a whole lot like it did at the beginning of the season, so, yeah, definitely, I was treading water. I was making more money from my two part-time gigs in the off-season than I was in my umpiring "career," but I didn't care. I wouldn't have traded my life for anyone's at that point. Well, strike that: I wouldn't have traded it for anyone's outside of baseball. Part of me was still thinking I could be playing, still wondering what might have been, but this was the next best thing. This was me, throwing in on a game I loved in the only way I could, and I was just loving the heck out of it. The rhythm of the road, the long slog of the season, the hopes and dreams of all these kids on the way up . . . it was all so damn exciting, so damn cool. And there I was, a part of it. Told myself I didn't mind the nothing pay, the grueling schedule, because I was still in the game.

I was doing great, really. And one of the reasons for this was my partner. When you're umpiring in the low level minors, your partner is everything. It's like a marriage. You're together

24/7. You share the same car, the same hotel room, everything. It's like you see on those cop shows on television, or in the buddy movies on the big screen. Your lives, your fortunes, your hopes and dreams . . . they're all intertwined. We were living out of my car, trying not to get on each other's nerves, living, breathing, sleeping baseball. We wouldn't actually *sleep* in the car, mind you, although we met our fair share of umps who did just that. No, we always had a room, but everything we owned was in the car, everything we needed. We knew each other like we knew ourselves.

Like I said, Jim had it wired. There were ten teams in the Midwest League, so that meant five sets of umpires—ten guys scrambling to make it to the next level—and we all compared notes. We were competing with each other for the attention of our supervisors, but it didn't feel like a competition. We helped each other out. If one set of umps got a good rate at a decent hotel, they told the rest of us and we made sure to get the same deal. If one of us found a place for a nice home-cooked meal, we made sure to send our friends around. Same with finding a decent place to do our laundry or a reliable mechanic. We were our own little network, and we checked in with each other constantly. And if one of us got called up, the rest of us heard about it double quick. We'd be happy for him, really and truly, but then we'd start in wondering why he'd gotten the call instead of us. And on and on.

Jim got promoted ahead of me, in the middle of the 1978 season. A job opened up in the Texas League and the call came to him. Don't think there was an ounce of jealousy running through my veins over Jim's good turn, because I knew he deserved it, and I knew my turn was coming, but I was a little anxious about teaming up with a new partner. It was the way of the game, but this was my first midseason shift, so it had me worried. Jim and I were a good team. We got along; we had each other's backs, fronts, sides . . . all around. I didn't think I could ever feel so comfortable with another partner, but I trusted that the road and the game would help me to make it work with whoever came my way next.

The thing is, Jim nearly didn't make it out of town. His last game, we were working in Appleton, Wisconsin. He was the driver that year, since I'd done the honors our first season. He had a Toyota, so we weren't exactly styling, and there wasn't a ton of room to stretch out or to stow our gear. The plan was for Jim to store his car in Appleton, and it worked out that my new partner, the guy they were calling up to replace Jim, was from the Appleton area, so we would use his car the rest of the season. The new guy's name was Phil Janssen, and we ended up getting along pretty well. Happily, he drove a long-boat Cadillac, so I could finally stretch my legs on those long hauls between games.

A bunch of us went out drinking after Jim's last game. We had some friends in Appleton by that point, because we'd been through town a time or two, and we got together over beers to give Jim a grand send-off. He parked his car on the street, out in front of the bar, but just before closing time some guy plowed into it. It didn't even look like a car when we stepped outside to see about all the noise: just a heap of glass and twisted metal. Completely totaled. And the worst part of it was that all of Jim's personals had been in the trunk and in the backseat. My stuff was back at the hotel, because I was staying on, but we had to sift through all of that glass and debris and fish out Jim's umpire gear bag, and his luggage, and his loose ends. And it took a good long while. For a couple beats, it felt like Jim would never get out of there. Felt like maybe this was some kind of sign.

Finally gave up the ghost on my playing career the following season, 1979, but not before making one last push. Turned out Phil Janssen was also a player. Jim Johnston was more of an official—a basketball referee, a football referee, a minor league umpire. But Phil was cut like me, hanging on to his baseball dreams, still thinking he could play, and when we got together we kind of stoked those last few embers.

We got into the habit of going to batting cages to pass the time on our travels. We'd make a game out of it, twenty swings for twenty balls, see who could make better, more consistent contact. It was just something to do for entertainment but it got us thinking more and more about playing. At night, after the games, we'd talk about this or that situation on the field, this or that player we'd just seen, and put ourselves in that same spot. You have to realize, a lot of these kids passing through the Midwest League were just out of high school. We thought we could still play with them, even though we knew full well that the further we moved away from playing the tougher it would be to get back to it.

Basically, we shared the same dream, and we were around dozens of kids every night who also shared that same dream, so it was tough to give up on it. It was all so *right there.*

One night, it was close enough to touch. We were in Wisconsin Rapids, working a series for the Wisconsin Rapids Twins, where a journeyman catcher named Rick Stelmaszek was the player-manager. He's now the bullpen coach for the Twins, so he's turned out to be a real lifer, but back then he'd been up and down the ranks, and he'd been managing in the Midwest League for a couple seasons. We used to sit around after the games, talking baseball, and since Rick was more of a player than a manager he was always asking specific questions about rules and interpretations and such. That's how it goes a lot of times. Players know the basics, they've been around the game their entire lives, but they don't know the intricacies. They don't know baselines, interference, obstructions . . . stuff like that.

Anyway, Rick always seemed to appreciate the tutorial, and I always appreciated the chance to get a grunt's perspective on the game, so it all worked out. We got along pretty well, and he was one of those guys I'd seek out whenever I saw his team on the schedule.

Turned out Rick had a catcher that year named George Dierberger, and we got along pretty well with him, too. Phil and I were tossing the ball around one day, and he said something about my arm that George happened to overhear. Said there was still a lot of pop in it. Said I should think about making a comeback. We were just kind of goofing around, but then we started to talk about it. Phil said, "No, really. You can still pitch."

Next day, George met us at a park in town and I threw to him from a mound. Threw for about a half hour, and I was still bringing it. There was good movement on my ball. A lot of hop on my fastball. All in all, it was a decent workout, and at the end of the session George was pumped. In fact, he was so pumped he went back to the ballpark that night and told Rick Stelmaszek about it. He said, "Skip, I think this guy can play."

This put Rick in a difficult spot. He could see I was still pretty athletic. He could see I had a love for the game. But he wasn't in any kind of position to give me a tryout or offer me any kind of real shot. He took me out for beers after the game that night and laid it out for me. He said, "Hate to break it to you, Jim, but you're an umpire. You've been out here two, three years calling games. You haven't pitched since college. I'd have to bring somebody in to watch you. I just don't think it's gonna happen."

Five or six beers in, I began to take his point, but it was a real fork in the road moment. I'd been nursing this dream for a long time, keeping it on life support, but I realized that night I'd have to let it go. Yeah, in the back of my mind, I knew I could compete at this level, but it took hearing this from Rick and airing it out on that mound with George Dierberger for me to finally realize it wasn't just about competing at this level. It was about getting to the next level, and the one after that. Realistically, I didn't have a shot. Not as a player. Just wasn't in the stars for me. But as an umpire, I had a pretty good chance of making it. All I had to do was keep doing what I was doing.

GAME

ARMANDO GALARRAGA

Like a Video Game

The first batter for Cleveland is the center fielder, Trevor Crowe. I do not know too much about this batter, only that he started the season in Triple A, like me. This only means he has a lot to prove, like me. I do not always like this, when another player is hungry. I like it when I am the only one who is hungry. Or when I am the *most* hungry. When my opponent is hungry it means he is playing with something extra. It means if you can beat him in a normal situation he will find a way to change the normal situation.

I throw Trevor Crowe a fastball low and away to start the game. I tell myself that if he is going to beat me, he will have to beat me on my best pitch. On most nights, my fastball and slider are my best pitches. I cannot tell from my warm-up, but I am hoping my fastball will be my best pitch for tonight. For the second pitch, I throw another fastball for a ball, so already I am behind in the count. A lot of pitching coaches, they will tell you that the first pitch to each batter is the most important, but I do not always believe this is so. Sometimes it is okay to start with a ball out of the strike zone, but only for a purpose. But to start 2–0, with the first two pitches not really serving any purpose, this is not okay, so I am upset with myself. It is okay to pitch a batter inside to push him from the plate, or outside to make him reach, or to maybe trick him with a ball in the dirt, but it is not okay to only miss with your location. I do not like it when I am so far from my game plan after only two pitches. I do not like it when the game tries to slip away before you can get a good grip.

I am telling myself to throw strikes to this batter. I do not want to make his job easy for him, so I concentrate on throwing strikes. Yes, I have been concentrating all along, but now I am concentrating even more. Now I am super-concentrating, and I am able to find the outside corner with another fastball. I like this corner. Then I throw another fastball down and in. The batter cannot get around in time and fouls it to the left side.

Now the count is 2–2 and we are back to even. In some ways, it is like a fresh start, this count. It is like the game has not started, even though there is now a history with me and this batter. There is a story we are each trying to tell. We are in the middle and at the beginning, both.

Normally, after four straight fastballs, with a 2–2 count, I would throw a slider. But I am not feeling normal, so I throw another fastball. It feels good to me, my fastball, so I try for another and the batter hits a fly ball to our center fielder, Austin Jackson. He is my friend, Austin Jackson, and a very good fielder. I know as soon as the ball is hit that it will be no problem for Austin Jackson, and it is no problem. Anything in the air, he can catch.

Now there is one out and the batter is Shin-Soo Choo. This is the man who is worrying me, and the worry makes me throw a fastball low and inside. I am frustrated, starting the first two batters behind in the count. But I come back with another fastball, low and away, and the umpire calls it for a strike. It is the same pitch I threw to the lead-off batter to get my first strike against him, so I am beginning to notice this. A lot of times, you do not get that call from the umpire, but the umpire tonight thinks this is a strike so I will keep going to the same place. Most umpires, in the first few innings, they tell you what they will do for the whole game, and once they tell you that is how you must pitch. Whatever they give, you must take.

Now, for the first time, I shake off my catcher. I have thrown seven straight fastballs and now Alex Avila wants me to throw a slider. It is probably a good call but I am not ready to throw a slider, so I tell him *no* with my head. He asks for it again with a sign, so I tell him *no* again. I want to throw my fastball. More and more, I am liking my fastball, so that is what I throw and Shin-Soo Choo can only hit it on the ground to Miguel Cabrera at first base. I have to run over to first base to make the play, like we practice in spring training. All the time, we practice this. My friends on the Tigers, they will say I am not such a good fielder, but I like to make this play because you get the batter out yourself. As a pitcher, this is the only chance I have to do this. Even when I get a strikeout, it is the catcher who is making the out—he is the last one to touch the ball. So I like to be the last one to touch the ball.

For the third batter, Austin Kearns, I only need one pitch. It is another fastball and he hits a line drive to Cabrera for the third out. He hits it good, but it is right at Cabrera, so it is an easy out. It is also a little bit lucky, because it could have been a base hit, a hit like that. The batter hit it hard, but he also hit it straight, right into Cabrera's glove.

I come off the field feeling happy. I am thinking, *One-two-three*. I did not throw too many pitches. I only threw fastballs. I did not get into any trouble. I still do not feel strong or dominant and I still cannot say if I will pitch one of my best games, or just an average game, or maybe even if I will struggle. I do not feel anything special, only that it is a good start.

Fausto Carmona is pitching for Cleveland. He is a good Dominican pitcher, with a good contract. Sometimes he can be very effective, like when he pitched against the Yankees in the play-offs. He works quickly when he is pitching, and I like this very much. It means that I can also work quickly. It means that if I have a good rhythm, if I am pitching well, I do not have to sit too long in the dugout. I do not have a chance to cool off or lose my rhythm, so it helps me to keep my focus. For Carmona, I am sure it is the same. We will match each other, quickness for quickness. If I work fast, if I do not throw too many pitches, it will help him to keep his rhythm, his focus. I want to pitch my game, but I do not want to help the other pitcher too much, and in the same way he does not want to help me.

We cannot do anything against Fausto Carmona in the bottom of the first inning. It is one-two-three for us, too, and Carmona throws only eleven pitches, so I am walking back to the mound almost before I can even sit down. But this is okay, because it is only the first inning, and because Cleveland goes one-two-three again in the top of the second. It is like we are taking turns. One-two-three, one-two-three. Like a dance.

The second inning, I start with two fastballs against Travis Hafner, the cleanup hitter. The first one has a nice sink and is called for a strike. The next one is up in the strike zone, which is not what I want, but Hafner can only foul it off. At 0–2, I throw another fastball, and Hafner chops a ground ball over the mound, which the shortstop fields, no problem.

Then, to the third baseman Jhonny Peralta, I throw another sinking fastball on the outside of the plate for a called strike. The second pitch is another fastball, and he fouls it off. Now I start to feel pretty good, like I am in control. For the first few batters, I have been seeing how I feel, but now I start to believe I have good stuff. Now I decide I will throw another fastball but I drop down with my delivery. Instead of throwing from the top, like my father used to teach me, I throw from a three-quarters delivery. Instead of at twelve o'clock, my arm is at ten o'clock. I do this sometimes, to make the batters guess what I will do. It is not good if they feel too comfortable. For the first five batters I have only thrown fastballs, so I think I will give the Cleveland hitters a different look. I do not want to stop throwing fastballs, only to change how I throw them, only for this next pitch.

The catcher, Alex Avila, only knows that it will be a fastball. That is all we are talking about with our signs. He makes the sign for a fastball, and I nod my head to show I am in agreement. So it is a surprise to him when I drop down and throw. It is a different look for him, too. It is also a surprise because my location is not so good, but I think Jhonny Peralta is uncomfortable, unfamiliar with the change in my release point, so he hits a soft pop-up to our second baseman, Carlos Guillen.

A lot of pitchers will throw a pitch out of the strike zone when they are ahead 0–2 in the count, but I do not like to do that. To me, every pitch is important. I believe this is true for me more than it is for other pitchers. Why? Because I am not a power pitcher. Sometimes I have very good velocity, but I need to throw strikes. A lot of pitchers, when they are 0–2 on a batter, they want to make the hitter swing at a bad pitch, but I only think what will happen if they do not swing at the bad pitch, because then it is only a bad pitch. Then it is a waste and I have given the hitter an advantage.

Also, early in the game, I do not want to go very deep in a count to a hitter. This is something I am thinking about as I look in to Alex Avila for the sign: another fastball. If I have a chance to get someone out on only two or three pitches, I will take that chance, especially early in the game. The hitter will come up to bat again later, and then again after that, so I like to get him out before he sees me make too many pitches, because every pitch he sees gives him information he can use for later.

Okay, so now there are two outs and I am feeling very good. I am facing Russell Branyan, the first baseman. He is a left-handed pull hitter with a big swing. I know about his swing from our meeting with the catcher and the pitching coach before the game, but I also know this from watching him. He is a big man, and he has a big swing, so for the first pitch I throw a fastball to that same corner, down and away. It is where the home plate umpire Marvin Hudson has been giving me the call. He is giving, so I will take. Then I go to the same corner again with another fastball, but this time Russell Branyan reaches across the plate and hits a foul ball back into the stands. I like that he does not take this pitch, because it means he is seeing what I am seeing. He knows the umpire will say it is a good pitch.

For the third time this inning, I am ahead 0–2 on the count, so I try to find that same spot with my next pitch, another fastball, only this time I do not get the call. I am not too worried about this, because I still like that corner. Maybe I just missed with that one, maybe just by a little bit. Against a left-handed hitter, down and away, that is still my corner, so I try for it again and the batter can only pull it softly on the ground to the second baseman, and now when I walk off the field I am feeling very strong, very positive. I am feeling like I can put the ball wherever I want it.

Miguel Cabrera leads off our half of the inning with a home run to left field. It is almost like a line drive, this home run. He hits the ball so hard, it leaves the stadium so fast, I can only be happy he is on my team. I am happy he has put us ahead, and that it was only one swing of the bat. Always, when I am pitching, I think about how long I am sitting in the dugout between innings. This is a secret most pitchers do not like to talk about. Yes, we like it when our team scores runs, but we do not always like it when we make the other pitcher throw a lot of pitches because it takes us from our own game. So I do not mind it so much when Carmona starts to focus much better after the home run. I am not rooting against my teammates, but I am anxious to get back onto the field. And very soon I have this chance. Carmona gets the next three batters, one-two-three, so once again I am back on the mound, only now we have a 1–0 lead.

This is okay, I think, because maybe one run will be enough. I am like a soccer player with the way I think. In soccer, if you have a good defense, sometimes you play for just one goal. When you score, it changes the personality of the game for your team. You switch to a defensive game, and you know that if you do not make a mistake the other team will not score. You know the game is yours. This is how I am feeling, like Fausto Carmona made a mistake to Miguel Cabrera. In baseball, you do not play for just one run, but sometimes that is all you need. When you are pitching well and you are not making any mistakes, you feel like you can keep the other team from scoring. A part of you wants your team to score more runs, but another part wants them to hurry up so you can get back on the mound and keep pitching.

Mark Grudzielanek is the leadoff hitter for Cleveland in the third inning. He is a veteran player. I have pitched to him many times. He was in the lineup for Kansas City when I pitched the six perfect innings in my rookie season, so he knows some things about me, the same way I know some things about him. In the meeting before the game, we talked about how he is a very smart player and very good at getting on base. I think about this as I step off the mound and put my face in my hat and kiss the word *Rinoceronte* for motivation. I tell myself I do not want this hitter to get on base. It is not because I expect to keep all of the Cleveland hitters from getting on base for the whole game. It is only that I do not want this leadoff hitter to reach. The reason for this is that when your teammates score a run for you as a pitcher, they tell you to put a zero on the board after they score. It is a way to keep the momentum, to keep the other team from scoring, so this is why I am thinking so hard about keeping Mark Grudzielanek from getting on base. If I give him a walk or a hit to start the inning there is a good chance he will come all the way around the bases.

I am not too worried about this, though. I am only just the right amount of worried. I start off with a fastball for a strike, only it is not the good kind of strike. It is right down the middle, straight, and I think the only reason Mark Grudzielanek does not swing at it is because he is looking for something else. He can see I am only throwing fastball, fastball, fastball. Away, away, away. So he does not expect this. Maybe he is thinking I will throw a slider or a changeup. And maybe he is still thinking this, so for the next pitch I follow with another fastball, down, and he can only lift an easy fly ball to Austin Jackson in center field.

To Mike Redmond, the Cleveland catcher, I fall behind a little bit. First I throw a strike to my favorite place for this umpire, only now because it is a right-handed hitter it is down and in. But then I miss with two pitches. One is the first pitch of the game to really get away from me. Alex Avila has to reach for it, it is so far outside. The other is inside, and now I am behind in the count, so I make sure my next fastball is for a strike. Mike Redmond is expecting this, but he can only hit a slow ground ball to deep short. It is not an easy play for our shortstop Ramon Santiago to make, but it is okay because Mike Redmond is not such a fast runner. A faster runner, maybe he would beat this play to first base, but it is not a problem.

The last batter in the Cleveland lineup is a young player named Jason Donald. He is also hungry, so I am careful to throw him a strike he cannot reach, on the outside corner. But then he goes with my next pitch, a fastball away, and he hits a nice line drive down the right field line. At first I am thinking it is a double, because he hits it really well, and it is falling away from the right fielder, but then I look up and see it is landing just outside the foul line. It is foul by only a few inches, so I am lucky. He is hungry and I am lucky, and for this one swing lucky is better than hungry. But I do not think lucky will always win, so I throw him a ball outside and hope he is so hungry that he swings at it. Normally, when a player is hungry, he is very aggressive, but Jason Donald does not like this pitch so he does not swing. It tells me he is hungry and at the same time he is smart. He is thinking.

Alex Avila, he is thinking, too. He shows me the sign for a slider, and this time I do not shake him off. For the first three innings, all the way through the Cleveland lineup, I have thrown only fastballs. I do not think I have ever started a game in this way, but for this game it feels like how I must pitch. Only now, after twenty-eight pitches, I agree that it is time for a slider, and Jason Donald is a little surprised. He swings, but he is a little surprised, and he hits an easy ground ball to shortstop for the third out.

Now I walk off the field like I am in total control. One-two-three, three times. It is a good way to start the game. It is a strong message, because the Cleveland hitters are frustrated, I can see. Jason Donald, with that line drive down the right field line, he thought he was having a good at bat, but in the end he could only hit a soft ground ball, so he is angry with himself. We walk off the field together and we are at opposite ends of our feelings. He is mad and I am glad and this is an important difference. It will give me an edge, this difference.

The other Cleveland players, they see this, too. My teammates for the Tigers, they also see this. It is like each side has its own body language and we are all listening, listening, listening.

For the middle innings, I have to face the same hitters all over again, so I tell myself again I must throw strikes, only now I must also mix up my pitches. I have thrown the first pitch for a fastball strike to seven hitters in a row. This is important. But now I have to be a little bit different. I have to throw my changeup. I have to throw my slider. I have to move the ball around. And so I do these things and I keep getting outs. In the fourth inning: groundout, fly ball, strikeout. In the fifth inning: foul out, groundout, groundout. Sometimes the Cleveland batters hit the ball hard and my teammates must make a good play behind me. Sometimes they do not hit the ball hard at all.

One-two-three, one-two-three. I am keeping the dance going. I am keeping the rhythm. The only trouble I have is in the fifth inning. It is only a little trouble, but it is big by comparison. When you are halfway through a game with no problems, you will notice even a small problem. It starts against Travis Hafner. With him, I miss with a lot of pitches. I do not miss by much, but I miss. I start out behind, 2–0, and then he gets to a full count. It is the only full count of the game, the only three-ball count, but I get him to fly out in foul territory so it does not matter.

The other trouble comes against Russell Branyan, with two outs. I do not pitch him inside, because he is a pull hitter, so I am trying to pitch him away. Then, on a 1–1 pitch, low, he grounds the ball back to the pitcher's mound. I am not in a good position to field this ball because I am turned around from my pitching motion, so the ball hits my foot before I can get my glove down. Then it bounces into the glove of our third baseman, Brandon Inge, who picks it up and throws to first to make the play. It is very lucky that the ball bounces off my foot in just this way. It is almost like magic. No, it was not hit hard, this ball, but it could have gone right up the middle, or it could have bounced to where no one was standing. It would have been a lucky hit, but now it is a lucky out. There is luck on both sides.

The whole time, we cannot do anything against Carmona. We cannot get a rally. In the dugout, I am starting to think it would be good to have another run. In baseball, one mistake can cost you a run, and it is possible I will make a mistake so I would like a cushion. Two runs are better than one, after all. Three runs are better than two. And four runs are the best of all. More than that, some pitchers get too relaxed. They lose some of their focus, because every pitch, every batter is not so important. They are not trying to do something special, something on purpose, with every pitch. They are only pitching. And here is another thing: too many runs will take too long for us to score. Right now the rhythm we have is excellent for my game. It is helping me. Carmona is getting a lot of quick outs, and this is helping me, too. So I am split between wanting more runs for a cushion and not wanting to lose the rhythm of the game.

I am not thinking yet about a no-hitter or a perfect game, but now I am starting to think about a shutout. What I am thinking about, exactly, is a complete game shutout. This would be a very big accomplishment for me, so I start to think this could be my night for a complete game shutout. This becomes my goal. In the front of my mind, all I am thinking is, *Keep it close, Armando. Keep the game close.* In the back of my mind is the complete game shutout. I am thinking how important it would be for my career. I am still proving myself and this would prove a lot.

I do not think of myself as a selfish player, but this is a selfish wish, I realize. For the team, I can only wish for a win. For me, I am wishing for something else, something more, so I do not like to admit that this is a part of my thinking, but I must be honest. I must tell what I was thinking.

For the sixth inning, Grudzielanek is leading off, so I throw him two straight sliders. The first time up, he only saw fastballs, so now he does not know what to expect. The first slider is called for a strike. The second is tailing away, very far outside, only he cannot help but swing. It is almost like a wild pitch, but it breaks late. It looks good and then it does not look good, but by then it is too late, so now Grudzielanek is uncomfortable. Then he fouls off a third slider and his shoulders sag. He is very frustrated. From his body language, I can tell that I have this guy. I want to point and say, "Hey, I got you." It is like he is already giving up, so I throw him a pitch outside. Maybe he will swing at it and miss badly and when he comes up the next time he will remember this and be even more frustrated. I am not only facing him for this at bat but also for the next at bat. But Grudzielanek does not swing and now it is one ball and two strikes. For the next pitch I come back over the plate, down and away, and he starts to swing and then tries to stop, so the umpire calls him out, and I watch Grudzielanek walk to the dugout very angry about this. It is good for my motivation to see him so upset. It is good for me and bad for him.

For the whole game, it is good for me and bad for them. I am in control. This is the key, the command of my fastball. It is like a video game. I can push the button and keep going to that corner, no problem. I can tell my fastball where I want it to go. Even if I am behind 2–0 I am not worried, because I know how to push the button.

I get the next two batters on easy fly balls. It is another quick inning, only eight pitches, so now I go back to the dugout and for the first time I think about the no-hitter. And it is not just the no-hitter, because I know nobody has reached base, so I think about the perfect game, too. Sometimes you will hear a pitcher say he did not know he had a perfect game but this cannot be so. As a pitcher, you know if you are pitching from the stretch, which a pitcher will do if there is someone on base. Tonight, I know I have not pitched from a stretch, so that is how I know nobody has reached base. That is how I know it can be a perfect game.

Here is when the game starts to feel special, different. To throw a perfect game, you need to have a lot of luck, and already there have been some lucky plays. There was the line drive to Miguel Cabrera. The foul ball down the line from Jason Donald. The grounder up the middle that bounced off my foot. I feel like all that luck should be for a reason, and I would like it very much if the reason is for a no-hitter or a perfect game.

I think, *Maybe I will need some more luck.*

Now I am excited and I am trying not to show that I am excited, both at the same time. To go through the lineup without allowing a single base runner, and then to go through the lineup a second time the same way, this is a very exciting thing, and now I must start thinking about one out at a time. To get twenty-seven outs in a row, it is almost impossible. You cannot think this way as a pitcher. But to get just one out, it is no problem. One out, you can always get, and then after that you can get one more, so I think ahead to the rest of the game and tell myself it is just one and one and one until we are finished. That is all.

We still cannot get anything to happen against Carmona, so I am back to work right away. I have an eight-pitch inning, one-two-three, and he has a seven-pitch inning, one-two-three. We are back and forth for the whole night. So now it is my turn, at the top of the seventh inning, and I have a six-pitch inning, one-two-three. All strikes. Groundout, fly out, groundout. The fans, they start to go a little crazy after this inning. They know I am close to a no-hitter, to a perfect game. It is not such a big crowd but they are making noise like a big crowd. They are standing, cheering, waving. I do not like to look at the crowd when I am pitching, but tonight I look. There is so much noise, so much excitement. It is something you can feel, this excitement. In the dugout, on the field, everywhere.

In the bottom of the seventh inning, we have a rally. I think maybe I will need it, this rally. We have runners on first and third with only one out, but we cannot score a run. Carmona gets a ground ball and his infielders make a double play, so the game stays close. It is still 1–0, and I am feeling more and more like I would like to have a cushion. The American players, they call this "breathing room," and at first I did not understand this expression. But now as I throw my warm-up pitches before the eighth inning, I understand it. I am relaxed, but it does not feel like I can breathe. It is not that I am nervous, because I am still feeling in control. I am still feeling like I am playing a video game and I know how to push the buttons on the controls. But there is no time for a deep breath. There is no time to stop and appreciate this moment. Everything is happening very fast.

I start with another first pitch strike to Travis Hafner. This makes eighteen first pitch strikes, to the first twenty-two batters. I do not know this as I am pitching, but I count them later in the box score. Then, on a 1–1 slider, I get him to chop a ground ball to shortstop for the first out.

To Jhonny Peralta I throw a slider for a strike. Then he swings and misses at another slider, away. Then I throw a ball low, to set him up for my next pitch, a slider in the dirt. He swings and misses for strike three. It is only my third strikeout of the game, I find out later. I am surprised by this, because it feels like I have more. And it is only the first one from swinging. Kearns, he struck out looking. And Grudzielanek, he was trying to check his swing but the umpire said he went around. If I have to pick a number at just this moment I would guess that I have more than three strikeouts. When you are feeling confident and in control, it feels like you are striking everyone out, like they are swinging and missing every time, but this is not always so.

Next comes the pull hitter, Russell Branyan, and he takes the first pitch for a strike. Then I throw a bad pitch, a slider outside, for a ball. I wanted to throw it down, but it does not go down. It stays up. This can be a dangerous thing, when the ball stays up, but it is lucky for me that it stays outside. If it was inside, maybe Branyan would crush it, but he does not swing so I am okay. After this, Alex Avila calls for a slider but I shake him off. I do not want to throw a slider in this situation. I want to throw a fastball. But Alex Avila keeps putting down the sign for a slider, so this is what I throw. Down. Branyan swings and fouls it back, so now it is 1–2, and after that he can only hit a soft ground ball to second base.

Now I leave the field and I am not thinking so much about keeping it close. I am not thinking any more about the win or the shutout. I am not even thinking about a no-hitter. I am thinking only about the perfect game, because the perfect game comes with all of these things. It comes with the win, the shutout, the no-hitter, everything. It is like a full package.

* * *

We finally have a rally, but it almost does not happen. The bottom of the eighth inning starts like another one-two-three for Carmona, but when there are two outs my friend Austin Jackson comes to bat. Already he has two hits in this game. He is a .300 hitter, and superfast. I think maybe he can get on base and start a rally, and this is what he does. He hits a hard ground ball between the shortstop and the third baseman for a single, so I am hoping we can bring him around to score. I do not think I will need more than one run for a cushion, but it would be nice to have this one.

Then, on an 0–2 pitch, Johnny Damon chops a ball to the shortstop, Jason Donald. The shortstop cannot make the force play at second base, because Austin Jackson is too fast, so he throws to first for the last out of the inning. Only it turns out that Johnny Damon is also too fast. The first base umpire Jim Joyce says he is safe. It does not look to me from the dugout like Johnny Damon is safe, but I cannot complain. When you are on the good side of a close call, you cannot complain. You can only think this is another lucky thing. It will not help me for a perfect game, this luck, but it can help me for a win. It can help me for my confidence if we score another run and I can start the ninth inning with a bigger lead.

The next batter is Magglio Ordonez. He is very good at driving in runs, so I am thinking maybe he can get a hit for us and help me with my cushion, and this is what he does. He hits a hard line drive to right field, and Austin Jackson comes around very fast to score. Johnny Damon also scores, but not so very fast. He only scores because there is a bad throw, so now we are winning 3–0 and I am thinking this will be my cushion. It will help me to relax, this cushion. It will give me my breathing room.

But now I switch to the other worry for pitchers, the one I do not like to talk about. I do not want to stay in the dugout anymore. I am ready to pitch. Miguel Cabrera is at bat, and I do not want him to have a bad at bat, I do not want him to hurry, but I do not want to wait to finish pitching. I am worried that my arm will cool off. I am worried that I will lose my rhythm, my focus.

Maybe Miguel Cabrera is thinking the same thing, because he strikes out swinging to end the inning.

The Comerica Park fans, they are standing up for the ninth inning. They are crazy with excitement. I like this very much, how they are cheering for me. It makes me feel good, but I do not want to think about this too much. The fans, they are only trying to help, to show their appreciation, but I am trying not to listen. I do not want to lose my focus. My teammates know this, so they do not say anything to me. Normally, when you go out to pitch the ninth inning for a complete game, everybody pats you on the back and tells you, "Good luck!" They pat you on the butt with their gloves. Something. But tonight they do not do any of these things. They stay far, far away from me, because this is the superstition in baseball. A perfect game, or a no-hitter, you are supposed to ignore it. You are supposed to pretend like it isn't there.

But I cannot pretend. My teammates, they can pretend, but it is almost all I can think about. I do not like this, that it is all I can think about, so I try to concentrate on my warm-up and on the next three batters. As I walk out to the mound, I pound my glove and say, "Vamos!"

Let's go!

"Vamos!"

Come on!

I am pumping myself up, but I do not want to pump myself up too, too much, so for my warm-up I calm down. I only make easy throws, loose, back and forth to the catcher. I am trying very hard to think only of the next batter, Mark Grudzielanek. I am thinking how his body language was so weak on his last at bat, how he was so uncomfortable. I am hoping it will be the same for this at bat. I am trying to see in my mind how it will go.

After my last warm-up, I step off the mound and try even harder to keep my focus. I do this every inning, only now it feels like there is a lot to think about. When Alex Avila throws the ball to second base, I walk behind the mound and take off my hat, like I always do. I look at the word I have written on the inside—*Rinoceronte*—and I repeat it to myself. And then a second time, I say this word. Sometimes I only kiss the word, where I have written it into my hat, but now I am kissing and whispering, all at the same time. Now I am reaching for the word and message of the story with my lips and my voice, to make these things a part of me and how I am pitching.

When I put the hat back on I think this is the reason why I wrote down this word in this way. I am thinking if I can put this word *on* my head I can also put it *in* my head. I can put it in my head to be strong, like a rhinoceros. To prepare, like a rhinoceros.

Finally, Mark Grudzielanek comes up and I do not think he wants to face me again. He comes up swinging. For my first pitch, I throw him a fastball, only a little up and away, but it is like he has already decided to swing. No matter what I will throw, he will swing. And he hits it really good. It surprises me how good he hits this ball. How hard, how far. I think it even surprises Mark Grudzielanek. The only good thing is that it does not surprise Austin Jackson in center field. He is playing in, very shallow, but as soon as Mark Grudzielanek makes contact, he is turning and running as fast as he can to deep, deep center field. Oh my goodness, he is running so fast, so far. While he is running, I am thinking, *Well, Armando . . . this is the end of the perfect game.* I am thinking it is a lucky thing about our three-run cushion, because I can still get the win. I am even thinking that Jim Leyland will let me stay and try for a complete game as long as I do not let anyone else get on base.

But then another lucky thing happens, and this is the luckiest of all of the lucky things, all put together. Austin Jackson runs and runs and the ball stays in the air long enough for him to run under it. He makes the most incredible catch. The most impossible catch. He makes this catch over his shoulder, running away from home plate. It is like the famous catch

made by Willie Mays. If you play baseball, if you watch baseball, you have seen this catch. Right away, I am thinking this
is a catch they will play over and over on ESPN, like the catch
by Willie Mays. It is so unbelievable, this catch. And I am so
unbelievably happy. Oh my goodness, I am standing behind
the mound, watching this, and I am smiling, smiling, smiling.
The fans, they are jumping up and down. My teammates in
the dugout, they are jumping up and down, too.

As soon as Austin Jackson makes this catch, I know I will
pitch a perfect game. I know this in my heart, in my bones. A
play like this, so much good luck like this, it can only happen
for a reason, and I tell myself the reason is for baseball history.
It is like it is my destiny to pitch this perfect game. This catch
by Austin Jackson, it has made it so.

Now I only want to hurry up and finish. I want to take
the excitement everybody feels about this catch and use it
for momentum for the next two outs. The next batter is the
catcher, Mike Redmond. He does not look very happy to be
coming up to bat, and I am glad to see this. Already I think I
have an edge, and even if this is not true it helps me to think
in this way. I throw another first pitch strike, a fastball away.
Then a slider out of the strike zone. At 1–1, I get a fastball in
on Redmond's hands but it is like he is expecting it. He hits it
hard, foul, down the third base line, so once again I am feeling
lucky. I come back with a slider, away, and he can only get his
bat on it for a soft ground ball to shortstop.

Two outs.

Comerica Park, it is now going completely crazy. The fans
are cheering, waving, jumping up and down. In my heart, also,

I am doing the same. It is difficult for me to concentrate. I am still feeling confident, still in control, but I also know that the last two hitters have hit the ball very hard. Grudzielanek, with that long fly to center. And Redmond, with that hard foul ball. But I am not too, too worried about this. It is only something new to think about, and already I have too many things to think about.

Business as Usual

I can't say for sure when I know something's going on. On the one hand, I know right out of the gate, from the very first inning. It's my job to know. As an ump, you pay attention to every last detail. You've got no choice. Might not have any direct impact on the game, but you know the situation at all times. As an ump who also happens to be a former pitcher, I tend to be really on top of it in terms of balls and strikes and base runners. If a guy has a no-no going, if he's perfect, I pay attention to that sort of thing. But on the other hand, it's not something I'm even thinking about.

It's there and it's not there. It matters and it doesn't.

A perfect game, it's such a rare thing most baseball folks don't even think of it until way late in the game. Even when you just worked one with your crew a couple weeks earlier. First perfect game I ever "participated" in—in any way, on any level—was on Mother's Day 2010, out in Oakland. The A's pitcher Dallas Braden was throwing blanks against Tampa Bay all game long.

I was working second base, and the whole way through, I knew. Didn't really pay attention to it, but I knew. It was there and not there, all at once. There wasn't a whole lot of action down by me, nothing close, nothing controversial, but on some level it's like we were ticking off each out, each inning. Even in the early innings, it felt like we were headed someplace special.

Anyway, *I* could feel it. Dallas Braden, he was feeling it. The guys on my crew, they were feeling it, too. Same guys as today, only Todd Tichenor was filling in for Marvin Hudson.

Just a year or so earlier, in the last month of the 2008 season, I worked my first no-hitter, a weird neutral-site game between the Cubs and the Astros. There'd been a hurricane down in Houston so the game was shifted to Milwaukee, and Carlos Zambrano was untouchable for Chicago. He walked a guy in the fourth and hit a guy in the fifth, but other than that he was perfect. I was working first base, and I could feel that one, too. It was a home game for the Astros but the crowd was mostly Cub fans, and they were into it. They were feeling it. It's like everyone *knew*.

Same here on this night. Maybe it's because we've got perfect games on our mind, all around baseball. Roy Halladay, just this past weekend, pitched a perfect game of his own down in Florida for the Phillies, and now this kid pitcher for the Tigers, Armando Galarraga, he's just going crazy out here on the mound in front of the home crowd. He's feeling it, no question. By the third or fourth inning, he's feeling it. You can see it in the way he walks off the mound after each inning. He's throwing strike after strike, and you know he's got a bunch more in his back pocket.

Here's the thing, though: I can't understand why the Cleveland hitters are swinging. I actually take time to wonder about this. It's not like I'm rooting for any one outcome or another, but I like to know what's going on. Yeah, Galarraga is having a lights-out night. And yeah, it looks to me like the hitters don't have a shot, but at the same time they're making it easy for him. He's racking up these six-, seven-, eight-pitch innings, and they're up there hacking. The Detroit hitters, too, they're taking their cuts. Fausto Carmona, the pitcher for the Indians, he's also lights-out. Miguel Cabrera touches him up for a solo shot in the bottom of the second, but that's it. A couple hits here and there but the Tigers can't get anything going, either.

They're just taking turns, is all.

It's an old-fashioned pitcher's duel, the kind you don't see too often anymore. Gibson and Marichal. Jenkins and Drysdale. One of those. There've been a lot of strong outings this season, but not too many with both starting pitchers on the top of their games. Both guys working like they've got someplace else to be. Both sharp.

At one point I look up and notice the time. It's just flying. Only other game I ever worked that moved at this kind of clip was a Greg Maddux beauty in 1997. First year of interleague play, he pitched a 2–0, three-hit shutout against Doc Gooden and the Yankees. Threw only eighty-four pitches. Eight-pitch innings, nine-pitch innings, seven-pitch innings. Just a masterful performance, start to finish, and that's what this kid for Detroit has got going here. These Cleveland hitters, they can't touch him, but at the same time they can't seem to hang back and work a deep count, make him throw a few more pitches.

And Carmona is right there, too. His pitch count is also low. His command is also sharp, also damn near perfect. The Tigers are jumping on him, too, but nobody can get anything going on either side of the scoreboard. They're feeding off each other, these two pitchers. Pushing each other. It's like they're throwing down a challenge each time they step off the mound. Telling the other guy, *Better not make a mistake, because I'm sure as hell not making any mistakes.* Back and forth like that, all night long.

First close play of the night comes with two outs, bottom of the third, and it's not really a close play at all—but, hey, when the game doesn't come your way for almost an hour, you'll take anything. Indians shortstop Jason Donald sends a hard liner down the first base line. Soon as it leaves the bat, it feels to me like it might be trouble, but I turn and watch as it falls just foul. I'm in good position to make the call, but there's nothing much to call. Not the kind of close play you really think about as an umpire, because it's not really close. It's close in terms of inches, but there's no doubt. Still, it's the first chance tonight for me to earn my keep, so I signal that the ball is foul.

A couple innings later, Galarraga is on a real nice roll, and Cleveland catcher Mike Redmond rips a fly ball that Detroit center fielder Austin Jackson just drifts under and puts away, no problem, and for some reason this play gets me thinking front-and-center about a perfect game. All along, I've been aware of it—back of my mind, front of my mind, wherever— but now Jackson hauls in this fly ball and it starts to feel real. Don't know what it is about this one play, but it's like it points the game in a whole new direction. It's just the second out in the top of the sixth inning, and it's pretty much a routine play, but as the ball comes back to the infield I catch myself thinking, *Okay, boys. Looks like we're in for another sparkler.* Yeah, a part of me has been thinking this way for a couple innings, but now I'm thinking it more and more. Now I see a guy like Austin Jackson just glide underneath this fly ball and it feels to me like Galarraga's teammates will catch everything that comes their way. Now it starts to feel inevitable, like we're on the side of history all over again.

Bottom of the eighth, there's finally a bang-bang play at first. Another chance to earn my keep. Two outs, runner on first, Johnny Damon at the plate. Carmona gets him to 0–2, but then Damon hits a soft hopper up the middle and legs out an infield hit. At least it feels to me like he legs it out. Afterward, a couple people will tell me the throw might have beaten him, but I've never seen the replay. A lot of times, I'll look at a close call after the game, to see if maybe I've messed up, but after this game I'm not much interested in seeing how much I messed up. Once is plenty, believe me. By that point, the Damon play didn't much matter.

Anyway, at the time, in the moment, it feels to me like Damon beats the throw, so I fling out my arms and call him safe, and no one argues too much one way or another. That's always the barometer, how much they argue, and I don't hear much of anything from Cleveland first baseman Russell Branyan, and I don't hear it from anyone on the bench, so I figure I got it right and now there are runners on first and second for Magglio Ordonez, who drives a single to right field to put the Tigers up 3–0.

Doesn't take too long, this two-out rally. Doesn't change the pace of the game. Carmona throws a bunch of pitches, but he gets Cabrera swinging to finish the inning and Galarraga is back out on the hill for the ninth in no time at all. And here's where my intuition kicks in. My gut, my instincts . . . all that good stuff. Don't know what it is but I start to have this hunch that the game is coming my way, and that it might just take the long way around. I'm not quite sure what I mean by this at first, but deep down I start to think we're in for some fireworks, something spectacular.

First pitch of the ninth, I see what I mean. Grudzielanek drives a ball to deep, deep center field. The deepest part of the ballpark, just about. Austin Jackson tries to run it down, and at first it doesn't look like he'll ever get there. Either he'll run out of park and the ball will sail over the center field fence or it'll short hop the wall before he can get anywhere close to it. Don't think I've ever seen an outfielder run so hard, so far, to make a play, but somewhere deep down there's that hunch. That premonition. My head is telling me there's no way this kid can ever make the play, but in my gut I can see the ball land in his outstretched glove like nothing at all. It's impossible and inescapable, both.

It's where this game is headed, no question.

Jackson ends up making a sick, over-the-shoulder, basket-type catch, and the place goes completely nuts. I see it the whole way and I still have no idea how he does it. The fans are out of their heads. The Detroit bench, the guys on the field, everyone. You can play this game for fifty years and never see a catch like this, so folks are hopping up and down and clapping each other on the back and laughing. It brings the crowd such a rush of adrenaline joy, this one catch, and for a beat or two it feels like the whole stadium is riding a giant, thrilling wave. I look over and see Galarraga biting back a smile. He's like a kid on Christmas morning. Then I look around and see everyone is the same way, flashing each other these disbelieving looks. Even on the Cleveland bench. It's Christmas all over the stadium.

Next batter is the Cleveland catcher, Mike Redmond, and the kid's got no shot. The mood of the room, the energy, the momentum . . . it's stacked all the way against him, and Galarraga gets him to tap a nothing grounder to shortstop Ramon Santiago. I punch him out at first but there's almost no need to bother. The guy's out by fifteen feet.

Now the place is going completely nuts, but I look over to the mound and see this kid pitcher looking remarkably composed. It's an amazing thing to see, how poised this kid looks out there on the mound. He's not pumping his fist, or shouting out some stupid rallying cry, or even mumbling to himself. He's just . . . there. Focused. Completely dialed in. And as the Cleveland shortstop digs in at the plate I allow myself one final, fleeting thought. I think, *It's coming to you, Jimmy. It's coming to you.*

Three

ARMANDO GALARRAGA

Up and Down

It is easy to forget that baseball is a business. The fans, they do not always realize this. The players, too. When you are in rehab and fighting back from an injury you do not think about anything more than getting healthy. You want to play, that is all. You want to show that you belong.

This is how it was for me after my surgery, so I was very happy that I could pitch in 2005. That is all, just to pitch. I did not mind that my arm became tired at the end of the season, because I was now a prospect. I knew this because they showed my face in *Baseball America,* so I was happy to go home and rest my arm. I had thrown a lot of innings, so it did not make sense to pitch for *Leones*. Instead, I worked on my conditioning, my focus.

But then something happened to take away my focus. Well, I must be accurate. It was really two things that happened. The first was a good distraction, but even a good distraction can take away your focus. For me, the good distraction was that

Washington put me on its forty-man roster. They called to tell me about it after I was home in Venezuela and I was very happy. You must be careful, though, when you hear good news like this, because you cannot believe you have finally reached your goal. Yes, it is a big milestone for a player to make it to the main roster. It means you make more money, which is nice, but it also means the club thinks of you like one of the best players. It means you are a part of their plans for the future.

But then I got another phone call from the Washington Nationals that told me those plans had changed. This second call was a bad distraction. It came in early December, about a month after the first call. This time they said they had some difficult news to tell me: I had been traded. "We do not want to see you go, Armando," they said. "You have come so far with us. You will have a big future. But this is baseball."

I was not prepared for this phone call, either. It does not matter, for good news or for bad news, you are never prepared. For a few moments I was very upset. I could not even listen to any of the details. But then I got still another important phone call. It was like being on a yo-yo, up and down with good news and bad news. This call was from the Texas Rangers. It was the opposite of the call from Washington. "We are very happy to have you, Armando," they said. "You are an important part of this deal. We would not have made this trade if we could not get you for our team."

I went from feeling sad about being traded to feeling lucky, because it meant the Texas Rangers wanted me to pitch for them. It felt good to be wanted. People told me this was how I would feel if I was traded, but I did not believe them. I thought only that it would hurt my feelings, but then I realized there was another side to it: there was a business side, a practical side. Also, Texas had traded a very good player to get me: Alfonso Soriano. He was not just a very good player. He was a superstar. He made the all-star team every year. Already he had been traded for Alex Rodriguez, and now he was being traded for me and an outfielder named Brad Wilkerson and a pinch hitter named Terrmel Sledge. It was like an honor, to be traded for a famous player like Alfonso Soriano. I thought about this and realized I liked it very much. In the newspapers, it said that Texas did not think they could sign Soriano and that he would become a free agent, so they wanted some good prospects. This meant they thought I was a good prospect. This meant it was not only *Baseball America* or the Washington Nationals who saw me in this way. I did not think anyone else in baseball even knew my name.

The most exciting part about being traded for such a big player like Alfonso Soriano was that Texas now had big plans for me, too. They put me on their forty-man roster, too. I was relieved about this, but I was most anxious about making the major league team. Being on the forty-man roster meant I would go to big league spring training for the first time in my career, and I did not want to go just to be a visitor. I wanted to make the team, and now I would have a good chance.

This was only a little bit true, of course. Yes, there was a chance I could make the team, but it was probably not a very good chance. Even though there are twenty-five players on an opening day major league roster, there are not twenty-five chances to make the team. There are only a certain number of spots for rookies, a certain number of spots for pitchers. The manager and the coaches, all during the winter, they have their ideas about who will be playing. They are making plans, discussing all of the different possibilities. And so even before spring training started, before I threw a single pitch in a Texas uniform, I knew it would be difficult to start the season with the big club. But this was not something I could use for motivation, so I pushed it away from my thinking. I knew it and I did not know it. I told myself there was a big chance even though I knew it was only a small chance.

There was another thing that could have taken my focus that year, but it had nothing to do with baseball. It had to do with getting married. Very quickly, Christin and I had become close. When I heard about the extra money I would make on the forty-man roster, I became very excited because I knew we could use the extra money to help us get started. I tried not to think about this kind of thing when I was pitching, but I could not always separate one type of thinking from the other. There was my baseball life and there was my regular life, and they were connected. The more success and the more happiness I had playing baseball, the more success and the more happiness I would have all over my life.

Here I will tell the story of how Christin and I became engaged, because it is connected to how I became a major league baseball player. More and more, we realized we were going to spend our lives with each other. More and more, I paid attention to how much money I was making as a baseball player, because it was not just for me. It was for our future. You see, after we first met during the 2005 season in Savannah, Georgia, we kept finding ways to be together. She visited me and met my family in Venezuela. I visited her and met her family in Chicago. In the beginning, we did not speak so well to each other. Her Spanish was not very good and my English was not very good, but this did not matter.

I proposed to Christin at my parents' apartment in Caracas, on a little balcony where Christin liked to sit at night. She liked that there was a breeze, and that you could look down and see all the people, all the activity. I had been planning for this night. I had been saving for a ring, which I put in a special plastic box, which was almost like a safe. Before we sat on the balcony I put the box in a certain place, and then when we sat down together I made sure Christin noticed it. She said, "What is this box doing here?"

I said, "I do not know. I have never seen this box before." I was pretending to be interested. I said, "Maybe we should open it."

Christin tried to open it, but you needed to know the combination. She tried and tried. I was getting nervous as she was trying to open the box. I was sweating. I was thinking maybe this was not such a good idea, to make her frustrated before asking such an important question like if she would marry me. It was my friend's idea to do this, and I thought it was a good idea, but now I was thinking it was a mistake, so before Christin became too frustrated I took the box from her, like I was trying to help.

I said, "You want to marry me?"

She looked at me like I was teasing. She said, "Armando!" She said it like she was scolding me, but in a playful way.

I said, "I am serious."

She looked at me again and could see I was serious. She said, "You want to marry me?" We had talked about this, but she could not believe it.

Then I opened the box and showed her the ring and she started crying and crying. Christin is a very romantic person, and she thought this was a very romantic proposal, so maybe my friend was right to have this idea.

Now that I was on the forty-man roster, I made more money. I went from making about $1,000 every two weeks during the season, to making about $2,000 every two weeks during the season. It would change our lives, this money. It would help us to be together and to have a wedding and a honeymoon. We talked about where we would get married. Maybe in Venezuela, where my family is from, or maybe in Chicago, where Christin's family is from. Or maybe we would get married in some middle place. We would see. For the next few months, I would concentrate on baseball, and after that we would see.

As I have written, since the day I signed with Montreal, I did not think so much about money when I was playing baseball. It was not so important. I did not always even ask how much my salary would be. I just wanted to keep playing, to keep moving up, but now the money was important, too. Now I started to ask and pay attention, and there were many more reasons to work hard and prepare for the new season.

The Texas Rangers had their spring training in Arizona, which is very different from Florida. Arizona was very beautiful. I did not know anybody on the Texas roster but I did not mind. The other players were very nice, very welcoming.

There were no Venezuelans on the team but Texas had many Dominican players who became my friends. There was a pitcher named Frank Francisco, and Joaquin Benoit, who now pitches for Tampa, and Francisco Cordero, who is now the closer for Cincinnati. I was a rookie, so I was very shy, but it helped to have these other players, these other pitchers, even though we were not together very long. I was one of the first players cut from camp. Buck Showalter was the manager then, and he was the one who told me. He said, "Armando, we are happy to have you here in camp, but we are going to send you down. If you work hard, you will be back. I know we will see you again soon in a Rangers uniform."

A lot of these guys, they tell you the same thing. Over and over, it is the same thing, but with Buck Showalter it sounded like he was not just being nice. He was trying to motivate me, I think, but I also think he was telling me I was still a part of his plans. That is how I heard him.

I started that year in Double A, in Frisco, Texas. It was a very beautiful town, with a very beautiful baseball stadium. I was happy there, only I was not happy for long because of my pitching. I only threw about forty innings, and I could not get people out. My shoulder hurt. My elbow hurt, too, but it was mostly my shoulder. I could not throw with any power, and my arm was sore, sore, sore. The Texas Rangers, they were very concerned about my arm. I was on their forty-man roster, and they had just traded a very famous player to get me, so they wanted to take care of me, to make sure I was okay. They sent me for an MRI, but it did not show anything. Already, I did not trust the MRI because of what happened in Florida, but I went along with whatever the doctor said. Then they sent me back to Arizona for rehabilitation and after about a month my arm started to feel a little better, a little stronger, so I started throwing again. I threw in Low A, in Spokane, Washington. I threw in High A, in Bakersfield, California. But I did not make it back to Frisco, so I was worried about my progress. The people from Texas said not to worry. They said, "Do not rush. You are not here for just one season. You are not here just to pitch for us in the minor leagues. We want you to be healthy so you can pitch for us in the major leagues."

They calmed me down. It was different from how I felt with Montreal, because then I was just a young pitcher trying to make a good impression. Now I was a prospect, so I went home to Venezuela after the season and started working again with Henrique Riquezes, my very first coach. I went to his academy every morning and worked out with weights, elastic bands, whatever he had. Everything was exactly the same, only now there were a few more players. Henrique was getting a good reputation for working with young players. I did a lot of running. Soon my shoulder was strong. Soon my whole body was strong. Even my mind was strong, in a way that was new for me. The American players called this being *locked in,* and that is how I was feeling. By January I started to throw again and I was reaching ninety-three, ninety-four on the radar gun. This was very good velocity for me. This was how I was throwing before my surgery, so I went back to spring training feeling very good about my chances. Once again I did not make the team. Once again they were very nice to me when they told me I was going to start the season in Frisco, in Double A. They made it sound like a positive thing, and it was. Even I could see this.

I was happy to be back in Frisco for the 2007 season, because it was such a beautiful place, and I was happy that my arm was strong. After a while they called me up to the Triple A team, in Oklahoma City, so this meant the Texas Rangers were happy with my progress. Christin was with me a lot of the time during the season, and I was happy about this, too. I was throwing a lot of innings, and my earned run average was low, so I was having a good season. Some games, I needed to make adjustments. Maybe I would give up four or five runs, so I would talk to the pitching coach and work on some things and the next game I would pitch seven innings and give up no runs. I was always learning, always improving.

When the season was almost over, the players all started to talk about getting called up to Texas for September. In the minor leagues, this is one of your goals. Everybody said they were going to call up four players, and I started to think I would be one of those players. For the whole season, I had been hearing how they had big plans for me with the big club, so I started to believe it. It was probably a mistake, to believe these things, because September came and I did not hear anything. One day I realized I had not seen my friend Edinson Volquez, another Dominican player, and then I heard somebody say he had been called up and had already left. He is now a really good pitcher for Cincinnati, and he had already pitched in the big leagues, so I was not too sad about this. I was happy for him. He deserved it. But then I heard they were going to call up three outfielders, and this did not make me so happy. I wanted them to take more pitchers. I wanted them to take me, because I thought I deserved it, too.

The last game of the season, I had a strong outing. For motivation I told myself that this was my last chance to show Texas how I could pitch, and to convince them to call me up. When I left the game, I was proud of my performance. I had given the manager and the coaches something to think about. And then, after the game, the manager called me in to his office to talk to me. Of course, I got very excited. I started to think, *Yeah, I'm getting called up!* I could not think of another reason why the manager would want to talk to me in private.

But it turned out I should not have been so excited, because as soon as I sat down the manager said, "Armando, the organization needs you back in Frisco. They are in the play-offs. They need another pitcher."

The whole time, I thought I was getting called up, and instead I was getting sent down. I could not believe it. I tried to hide my disappointment from the manager, but I did not think he cared either way. He did not seem to understand why I would be so upset about this, or why he should even have to talk to me about my disappointment, but I did not think this was his decision. He was only telling me what someone else had told him.

I said, "Are you serious? I do not want to go down. I want to go up."

He said, "There is nothing we can do about it, Armando. The decision has been made."

I did not like this decision at all. Right away, I called my agent to complain about it. I felt like crying, but I would not cry. I felt like screaming, but I would not scream. I felt like kicking a chair, but I would not do that, either. I just called my agent and said, "I am not going."

He said, "Armando, do not do something you might regret."

I was supposed to take the next flight to Frisco. They gave me a ticket but I threw it in my bag without looking at it. I was very angry, very frustrated. I did not know what to do. The only thing I knew was that I did not want to go to Frisco. Yes, it was in Texas, so on the map it was closer to Arlington, where the Rangers played, but in reality it was farther away.

Next I called Christin and told her what had happened, and that I did not want to go back to Double A. She did not want me to make a bad decision. She said, "Armando, this is your career. You have worked so hard. You cannot throw away everything for the future just because you are disappointed for today."

This was good advice, but I could not hear it at that moment.

I did not know this at the time but my agent called my dad in Venezuela to get him to talk to me. All of the people in my life were telling me to forget about it, to go to Frisco like the Rangers were asking, but by the time I realized they were right I had missed the plane. This was a problem, because there were not so many flights between Oklahoma City and Frisco. The only way to get there in time for the first game of the play-offs was to drive, so that is what we did. Christin and I drove and drove, over four hours without stopping. She tried to talk to me about it the whole way there, but I did not want to talk about it. I did not want to go, but I was going, and I did not think there was anything to talk about.

I was supposed to pitch the second game of the play-offs. This was what they told me before I left. A friend of mine named Luis Mendoza was supposed to pitch the first game, but when I got to the stadium he was cleaning out his locker. He saw me and said, "Gala, you're pitching the first game after all."

I said, "What do you mean? You are pitching the first game."

He said, "No, there has been a change. They just called me up." He was smiling and not smiling as he said this, because he knew that his happiness was also my disappointment. He was my friend, so he knew this. We were moving in opposite directions, one up and one down.

I congratulated Luis, because it was not his fault that this happened, and because he deserved this chance the same way I deserved this chance, but I was hurt and confused by this news. I had just driven four hours to Frisco, from Triple A to Double A, going in the wrong direction for a baseball player. The only reason I did this was because the Texas Rangers told me they needed pitchers for the play-offs, and because everyone told me I should not throw away my career for a disappointment, and now that I was here I found out that one of the few pitchers they already had on the team was leaving to join the big club. It did not make any sense to me. I was already crying in my heart about being sent down, and then to see another pitcher being called up ahead of me made me want to cry even more.

But I was already there so I pitched. There was nothing else to do. I did not care so much if we won the game. I knew all of the players, but I did not feel so much like part of the team. I ended up throwing a good game. We lost, but my pitching was okay. I went seven innings and gave up two runs, but we could not score against a very good team from San Antonio. They were playing as a team, and we were just playing, so they beat us three games in a row. I did not make another start because it was a best-of-five series, so our season was over. We all packed our things. In my head, I was already thinking about Christin and our wedding and our future together.

After the play-offs, we drove to Austin to visit my sister. My mom and dad flew up from Caracas to join us. I was really looking forward to it. I did not like how my season had ended and I did not like how my career was going and I did not like how all these other pitchers were getting called up ahead of me, so I decided this would be a good distraction. We could talk about our wedding plans, and go into town and listen to music, and just relax. But I did not get a good chance to do any of these things in Austin. For a few days, yes, I started to forget about the season and all of my frustration, but then I got another phone call from the Texas Rangers. I was not expecting a call, because my season was finished. I did not think I would speak to anyone from Texas until spring training. But my cell phone rang early one morning while everyone else was still asleep. It was someone from the team, telling me to get the next flight to Detroit, where the Rangers were playing the Tigers.

I said, "Does this mean I am getting called up?" I was very excited, but the man on the other side of the phone was not so excited, so I wanted to make sure.

He said, "Yes." That is all. Just, *yes.*

I do not know why they changed their minds about calling me up, or if this had been the plan for me the whole time. They did not say, and I did not ask. I only know that I ran around my sister's house, making a lot of noise. My whole family was there, and we were all superhappy with this news. My fiancée was superhappy. We were all running around, screaming and laughing and celebrating. It was early in the morning for so much screaming and laughing and celebrating but the neighbors did not mind.

I did not want to miss this next flight to Detroit, because this time it would not be so easy to drive all the way from Austin, so I got my few things together and hurried to the airport. I went to Detroit by myself. We looked quickly at the Texas schedule and saw that from Detroit I would be going to Oakland, so Christin said she would try to meet me there.

In Detroit, I took a taxi to the stadium from the airport. I had never been to a major league stadium, and where the Tigers played was very beautiful, very new. I could not imagine that this was where I would be playing. Even the locker room was beautiful. It was not like a locker room at all, and I could not believe there was already a uniform hanging there with my name on it. There was a blue T-shirt there, too, and I put it on. This was the first thing I did, to make me feel like a big league ballplayer. Then I sat on the chair in front of my locker and tried to remember this moment. I sat there wearing my blue Texas T-shirt and thought, *Wow*. That was the only thing I could think, to come all the way from Venezuela with a dream of playing in the major leagues, and to finally make it. All along, this had been my dream, but I did not know if it could ever come true. For every hundred players, only one makes the big leagues. That is all, just one. It is not such a big number.

I did not pitch for my first two games in Detroit. I was in the bullpen. Once, the bullpen coach told me to warm up, but I did not get into the game, only I did not care. I only cared that I was there, in a big league uniform.

Christin flew with her mom to meet me in Oakland. Her brother also came to see me play. It was expensive to make such a trip, but we did not think about the money because now I was making a big league salary. Now I was making about $17,000 every two weeks, which was the minimum. Before, I did not make $17,000 for an entire season, so it was very exciting to look at my first big league paycheck—but I was more excited to look at myself in the mirror wearing a big league uniform.

I finally got into a game in Oakland, on September 15, 2007. I will always remember that date. It was the eighth inning. I was going to pitch against the Oakland A's, my favorite team from when I was a boy. I closed my eyes and imagined that I would be facing Rickey Henderson.

We were losing 7–3, so it was not such an important game. Both teams were having losing seasons. Both teams were out of the play-offs. But it was an important game for me. Our catcher, Jarrod Saltalamacchia, came out to talk to me before I threw my first pitch. He said, "Are you nervous?"

I said, "Yeah, I'm pretty nervous."

He said, "Do not worry. You will be fine."

And I was. I walked the first batter, the Oakland catcher Kurt Suzuki, but then I got the next three batters on only seven pitches. There was a fly ball to center field, a pop fly to shortstop, and a fly ball to left field. I was not happy about the walk to start my career, but I was happy with how my first game ended.

A few days later I pitched three innings in Minnesota. This time I came in to start the sixth inning. We were losing 3–1, so the game was a little closer. This time I had to face some very good hitters, like Justin Morneau and Joe Mauer. And this time I gave up a home run, to Jason Kubel, the designated hitter, but it was not such a bad performance. Three innings, one earned run.

Finally, the manager Ron Washington told me I was going to make a start in Texas against the Angels. I called everybody back home in Venezuela to tell them about it. They were all watching on television, all of my friends and family. It was a big moment for me, because Texas did not trade for me to be a relief pitcher. They traded for me to be a starter, so this was a very meaningful game. In the standings, it did not mean so much—the Angels were in first place, with a big lead, and there were not so many games left in the season—but for me it was everything. And for a few innings it was a big success. I did not allow a hit for the first four innings. A few walks, yes, but no base hits, but then I lost my focus. I do not know how or why this happened. Maybe I was so pleased with how I was pitching that I allowed myself to relax, or maybe my arm was getting tired. I do not know. All I know was that we were winning 4–0 and I had a chance to get my first win, but I walked Juan Rivera to start the fifth inning and after that I was in trouble. After that, there was a single, a double, a strikeout, a fly ball, another single, and a home run. That meant four hits and five runs. It also meant we were now losing 5–4 and I was out of the game.

In just one inning I went from feeling strong and positive to feeling embarrassed and frustrated. First I was up and then I was down. The pitching coach, Mark Connor, came over to me in the dugout after I was pulled from the game and said, "You okay?" He said it first like a question, but then when I nodded he said it again, like he was telling me something. He said, "You okay."

That is all he ever said. I did not get into a game the last week of the season. And Mark Connor, he did not say anything else to me the last week of the season. Even when I was throwing a bullpen session he did not say anything. He turned his back to me like he did not care one way or the other.

I tried not to worry about this. I was now a major league baseball player. That is what I kept telling myself, but I must now tell the truth: I did not start to feel like a major league baseball player until we were getting ready to leave Texas for our last road trip of the season. In baseball, there are a lot of rituals, a lot of traditions. When you are in the minor leagues you are always hearing about this. One of the stories we kept hearing about was how the veteran players make all the rookies do crazy things, like an initiation. It is a way for the old players to make the new players feel like part of the team, so this is why I did not feel like a part of the team right away. I was waiting for my initiation, and it did not come until we were finishing our season in Texas.

Here is what happened: I went to the locker room after our last home game and saw that all of my clothes had been taken away. This was a big surprise. The only thing in my locker was a ballerina costume. I saw this ballerina costume and I could not believe it. The other players, they were all laughing. The other rookies, all of the September call-ups, their clothes had been taken away, too. In Jarrod Saltalamacchia's locker were clothes for a baby. There was a giant diaper and a baby bonnet. In Edinson Volquez's locker were the clothes for a prostitute. For one of the other rookies, there was a costume for a waitress from Hooters.

Kevin Millwood was the veteran player on the Rangers who was organizing all of this. He was in charge, so he was laughing most of all. He told us we had to wear these clothes to the airport and on our flight to Seattle. We could not question this. Then we had to wear our costumes to the hotel and go out to a bar with our teammates. I did not mind this so much. Actually, I liked it, except that it was very cold when we got to Seattle, and I was only wearing a ballerina costume. I liked it because now I could feel like a part of the team. Now I could feel like a major league baseball player.

And so I was happy. I was disappointed with my start, with the way I lost my focus, but I liked wearing a major league uniform. I liked getting a major league paycheck. I liked that I was having my dream come true, but now I wanted a bigger dream. Now I wanted my pitching coach to talk to me. I wanted my manager to talk to me. I wanted someone to tell me what I should be doing to improve.

As soon as the season finished, Christin and I started making plans for our wedding. We decided we would have two weddings, one in Venezuela and one in Chicago. First, on January 19, we got married in Venezuela. Then we had a big party. My father has six brothers and my mother has six brothers, so I have a very large family. I have a lot of cousins, so there were a lot of people there.

Then we went to Chicago for a church ceremony on January 26 and another big party, only something happened that almost upset all of our plans. The night before, I was in the hotel in Chicago, getting ready, when I got another call from the Texas Rangers. I could not think why anyone from Texas would be calling, except maybe to congratulate me about my wedding, but this was not the reason. They were calling to tell me I was being put on assignment. I did not know what this meant at the time, but I knew it was not good. It meant that if Texas could not find another team to trade for me in ten days, I would be put on waivers. It meant my career might be over before it had even started.

I could not believe that I would get this phone call at a time like this, the day before my wedding. It told me I was not so important to Texas anymore. It told me why the pitching coach and the manager never talked to me after my one and only start. Yes, I was important to Christin. We were in the middle of getting married. But I was not important as a baseball player. I sat down on the bed and tried not to cry. Christin was with me and she made me feel a little better. She helped me to see that this was not the end of me playing baseball.

Together, we decided we would not tell anyone else about my assignment because we did not want to ruin the celebration. We did not even tell my father, because he was so excited to be in Chicago for the first time: so excited that I was getting married, so excited that I had made it to the big leagues. There were a lot of people who were very happy for me and Christin, and I did not want to upset them, so I tried to push baseball away from my mind and focus on my friends and family.

Underneath, I could not really enjoy myself because I was so worried about my career. Christin could see that I was worried but we pushed it away together. It was our first struggle as husband and wife, and it was a good thing and a bad thing. It was good that we had each other and it was bad that this was happening.

Somehow we managed to have a good time. There was a lot of food, a lot of drinking, and a lot of dancing. After the party we went on a cruise. It started in Puerto Rico, and we went to Barbados, St. Maarten, Aruba, all over. Once again, we managed to have a good time. Once again, there was a lot of food, a lot of drinking, and a lot of dancing. But together with that good time there was also a sadness. I kept worrying about baseball and wondering if another team would pick me up before spring training.

On a cruise ship, it is sometimes difficult to get cell phone service and Internet coverage. It is not only difficult, but expensive, so we did not always carry our phones or look at e-mail. Every few days, perhaps, we checked in to see what was happening, and finally we heard from my agent, who said the Tigers wanted to sign me and invite me to spring training in Lakeland, Florida. He said, "Now you do not have to worry, Armando. Now you can enjoy your honeymoon. Now everything will work out."

This was a big relief because it meant that now we could relax. Now we knew that I was still a major league baseball player.

JIM JOYCE

Catch/No-Catch

One of my favorite rituals as a minor league umpire was rubbing up the baseballs before a game. Well, maybe *favorite* is a bit much. Don't mean to make it sound fun or glamorous. It was tedious work, more chore than ritual, but I always thought it was a good way to get my head around the game I was about to call. Forced me to sit and focus on a simple task, and connected me to the way umpires had been preparing for a game for generations.

I'm not super-religious but it struck me as a kind of sacred rite. A testament to the game.

A lot of folks outside the game don't really know about this practice, but umpires have been rubbing baseballs with mud since the 1920s, to take the slickness and shine from them before putting them into play. A brand-new, out-of-the-box baseball can be a slippery thing, so major league teams use an expensive, hard-to-find compound called Lena Blackburne Baseball Rubbing Mud to make it so players can get a better grip. The mud comes from an out of the way creek in New Jersey, but the precise location of the mud bank is a closely guarded secret. Guys used to say they could tell me where it was but then they'd have to kill me. We made a joke out of it. For some reason, the mud from this area has just the right amount of silt and sand to take the edge off a baseball without taking the whiteness from it, so this is what we use—most minor league teams can't afford the stuff so those umpires make do with the dirt in the parking lot.

At the end of the day it's still dirt.

Nobody sits you down and teaches you about this kind of thing when you're starting out. You just watch the guy ahead of you and follow his lead. You improvise. Over the years, I developed my own mixture and it seemed to work pretty well. I'd take a cup of dirt from the softest, most gravel-free patch of soil I could find, usually from the parking lot outside the stadium or maybe from a flower bed outside my hotel. Then I'd add a little water and a shot of Coke. Gave it just the right consistency. Only problem with this recipe was the mud started to stink before too long. If you didn't remember to toss the mud when you were through, you'd come back and it would stink like a goat's ass. Man, that smell was fierce! But the mix really did the trick. Left the leather on those baseballs looking and feeling just right.

I mention this only to show how us minor league umpires got by. There were hard-and-fast rules, but a lot of times they weren't all that hard or fast. There are supervisors watching us, but they weren't really telling us what to do. A lot of this stuff we were left to figure out for ourselves.

All the way through Triple A, umpires have to go through these motions, rubbing up these baseballs. Still, to this day. If you're working the plate it falls to you, so each ump has his own special recipe, his own routine. Once you get to the bigs, the clubhouse guys take care of this, and most umps don't miss it, but from time to time I wish I had that little pocket of calm before each game, that little piece of busywork to force me to close out the rest of the world and focus on what I'm about to do.

Let me tell you, that night after Armando's near-perfect game in Detroit, when they had me working the plate, I could have used a good hour of mindless, tedious busywork to get me out of my head and help me get back to work. But that's a different part of the story.

For now, I'll just say that I caught up to my buddy Jim Johnston in the Texas League the year after he moved up there and we partnered up again, and from there things seemed to progress for me at a standard clip. I'd log my time at each level, usually with a new partner, get used to the slight bump in pay, and then I'd get promoted and try to make a name for myself all over again. From the outside looking in, you'd probably say I was making all the right moves on the field, going through all the right motions in my career. But there was a flip side to it, a down side. After a while, it got to where I was working so long, traveling so many back roads and sleeping in so many fleabag motels, I couldn't tell one season from another. One game seemed to run into the next, making one long string of innings that could stretch across the seasons. When you're a player, at least you get to break up your year with a couple long home stands. You get to stay in one place for a while, sleep in your own bed. But when you're an umpire every game is a road game, so it can get a little wearying after a while. You start to look for ways to break up the routine.

My first season in the Pacific Coast League, 1981, there was an unexpected blip in our schedule. Turned out to be a real game changer for me. We were in Portland, Oregon, about to drive up to Vancouver for a five-game series, but there was a garbage strike up there that basically shut down the whole city. The series was canceled and we were told to just sit tight in Portland while the situation sorted itself out and the league could reschedule those games. So for a couple days we had a nice little pause. And the way it worked out, that garbage strike changed my life. You see, while we were hanging out, twiddling our thumbs in Portland, a bunch of us were invited out to dinner. Now, I was never a big fan of these types of dinner invitations, which came with the territory in a lot of these minor league towns. Don't get me wrong, folks were as nice as nice could be, opening up their homes to us, wanting to get a little closer to the game, throwing us a little kindness. I never minded a home-cooked meal, especially in the middle of a long season, but I was a little uncomfortable around people I didn't know. I always appreciated the invitation, but most of the time it was an awkward evening of polite conversation with people I might not ever see again, so I usually declined. Politely, of course.

On this night, though, my partner Kirk Levine pressed me to join him at the home of his wife's aunt and uncle, who happened to live in Portland. It was a Saturday night and I had nothing else to do so I tagged along, and it was good that I did. For one thing, I liked our hosts immediately. Claud and Margaret Cochran, Kirk's wife's aunt and uncle, were tremendous people: fun, gracious, generous. Margaret put out a spread like you wouldn't believe. Turkey, mashed potatoes, stuffing . . . all the trimmings. And Claud was pretty liberal on the pour. We had drinks before dinner, during dinner, after dinner. And a whole lot of laughs, too. It was shaping up to be a perfectly fine evening and then it got even better because just as we were finishing up a beautiful blonde came in the front door. I turned to Kirk and whispered, "Who the hell is that?"

He said it was his wife's cousin Kay—the daughter of our hosts.

I was head over heels, right away. On her side of the room, Kay couldn't have been any less interested in me, but she was sweet about it. She sat with us around the fireplace for a bit and I gave her my full attention. Pulled out all the charm, but it didn't get me anywhere. After a while, I asked her if she wanted to maybe go out for a couple drinks later on that night, but she declined. Said it was late, she was tired, whatever. So then I offered her parents tickets to a game the following night, because the league had just moved those canceled Vancouver games down to Portland, and I asked Kay if she'd like to join. She hemmed and hawed, and then finally agreed, but only if she could bring her sister Carol along as well.

We ended up going out after the game and having a really good time, and we've been together ever since. It worked out that the schedule brought me back to Portland a bunch of times that season so I found myself looking forward to those trips and dreading each time I'd have to leave. Very quickly, Kay became my something to look forward to, my someone to come home to, and at the end of the season I packed up my few belongings from my parents' house in Toledo and moved out to Portland.

By the middle of the next season we were married. June 11, 1982. People always ask me how we picked that date, which was a Friday, which I guess was unusual. Simple: I had a day off. We got married in Kay's backyard. My parents came out with my brother for the wedding. Kay's sister was the maid of honor. My brother was the best man. Kay's dog, Dolly, was one of the flower girls.

The next day, my game was rained out, so we hung around and opened our presents. Then I left town for twelve days and poor Kay had to get used to the life of an umpire's wife, straight out of the gate. She knew the drill by that point. Hadn't been much of a fan, going in. Heck, she didn't follow baseball at all, but she understood the life she was signing on to. She accepted it. I just hated that she didn't have a chance to ease into it.

One day we were getting married. Two days later I was gone.

Jump ahead a couple seasons to 1986. I was still working the Coast League, still dreaming of a shot at the bigs. The money was a little better, but for the first time I started to think I might never get where I was itching to go. Each year, past couple years, that dream seemed more and more out of reach, to where I was starting to think I might never make it. Wasn't the same kind of low moment I'd had back in my first season, when I was missing home, but I was starting to have a couple doubts.

Most of these doubts had to do with money—specifically, me not making enough of it. We'd started a family and it was tough to stretch my $900 monthly pay to cover our bills. On top of my salary, I also drew about $55 in per diem money, which was, of course, meant to cover my hotel and food and car expenses. It was a generous amount for 1986, but the league set it up this way because it was better for us in terms of taxes. They picked up our flights, and we had deals with rental car companies in most Coast League towns. We made all the arrangements ourselves and put in for our expenses as we went along. What we couldn't afford, we'd wangle. We'd swap out tickets to the game for a rental car, sometimes for a hotel room or a meal. There was a lot of wheeling and dealing going on, and the idea was to pocket as much of that per diem as we could. I tried to send at least $1,000 home to Kay every month when I was on the road. It really helped when I had a stretch of games in Portland, though, I'll say that. For the first time in my career as an umpire, I had a real home stand to look forward to on the schedule, so my expense money went a little further for those games.

The rest of my doubts had to do with me not getting promoted. First couple years, this had been a far-off goal. Then it became a growing worry. Now it was an out-and-out concern. At that time in baseball there were two ways for an umpire to make it to the majors. There was an American League route and a National League route. There were two different league presidents, two different supervisors for umpires. Everything was split. The idea was for one of those supervisors to invite you to spring training. Out of that, if you made a positive impression, sometimes they'd give you a half-season schedule and sometimes they'd give you a full-season, but you'd take either one. Or maybe they'd see something they liked enough to call you back midseason, to fill in for any number of reasons. You just wanted them to purchase your contract. That was your foot in the door. After that, you could wedge yourself in the rest of the way.

I hadn't been to spring training at all, so that was my main goal. Just to get a long, fair look at the major league level. Guys were passing me left and right, and I kept getting sent back to the Coast League. Either I wasn't cutting it or these supervisors just didn't like me. One or the other. I'd never get any direct criticism or negative feedback, so there was no way to know. Just kept getting passed over by these guys with less seniority. Let me tell you, it was frustrating. And maddening. There was no one to tell me what I was doing wrong, what I was doing right, anything. All I could do was sit and stew. Had a whole bunch of friends in the game by this point, but for the most part they'd moved up and out and were working in the bigs. Or they'd drifted away from umpiring and into something else. In any case, their sympathies ran only so far. I could talk to Kay, but there wasn't a whole lot she could tell me. She was worried about my progress, same as me, but she was worried for different reasons. She was worried because she was working like crazy back home, because our son Jimmy was three years old, because it never seemed like we could get out from under.

Okay, so that's the setup. That puts you in my frame of mind, early August 1986. I was in Albuquerque. One of my partners had been called to the bigs, so that left us with a two-man crew. Typically, in Triple A, there are three-man crews: one ump behind the plate, one at first, one at third. There wasn't enough time left in the season to bring in another guy, though, so we just worked it short. We'd all come up that way: one ump behind the plate, one at first. No big thing. Except it was, because I wanted to be the one called up to the bigs after all this time. I wanted to be the guy leaving the two other umps behind. Five years is a long, long time to be working the same level, a long, long time to have to watch all these other guys make it up and out ahead of me.

Here's how long it was, exactly: there were twenty-six teams in Triple A at the time, spread among the Pacific Coast League, the American Association, and the International League. That meant no more than thirteen games on the schedule each day at that level, which added up to thirty-nine umpires. No more, no less. There was no need for subs, since if one guy couldn't make it due to sickness or injury, we'd just work short. We all knew each other, in a kind of, sort of way. We knew each other's strengths and weaknesses, and which of us were on a fast track to the bigs.

Can't say for sure, but I had about the longest tenure among this group, which is not really saying much. It's what's known as a dubious honor, kind of like that Kevin Costner character in *Bull Durham*. You hang around the minors long enough, you get to be the all-time home run leader, when all you really want is to just hit one dinger in the bigs. That was me back then. I just wanted my shot.

The supervisor for American League umpires at the time was a guy named Dick Butler, and he was coming to the stadium in Albuquerque to watch the game. A lot of times, you had no idea when a supervisor was coming, but if you were lucky someone would tip you off. I didn't know if Dick Butler was coming to check out me, or my partner, or if he was just passing through town. All I knew was that he was coming and that I needed to be on my game. Turned out it was a doubleheader and I had the plate for the first game. Turned out to be a three-and-a-half-hour game, which was on the long side for seven innings. (In the minor leagues, games are shortened to seven innings for doubleheaders.) Turned out that this was a giant red flag for someone like Dick Butler.

Now Dick Butler was a good guy, and a good judge of umpires, but he was all about moving the game along. That was his big thing, almost like a pet peeve. Sure enough, after the game, he came up to me to talk about this very thing. He said, "Jim, what took you so long out there?"

I said, "Mr. Butler, no disrespect, but there were ten pitchers tonight. Those pitching changes can eat up a lot of time."

He said, "Well, do you think you did a good job out there?"

I said, "Wasn't my best, but I think I called a good game, yeah."

And that was that. He just kind of walked away, made his disapproval known, and left me thinking, *Heck, that's not very fair*. And it wasn't. I mean, you bring a supervisor around to evaluate you, to judge you as a potential candidate for the major leagues, and to build it all on one seven-inning game just didn't seem right. It aggravated the crap out of me, if I'm being honest. But there wasn't a single thing I could do about it, so I tried to set my aggravation aside.

You have to realize, a call to the bigs would have meant the world to me and Kay. Forget what it might have meant to me personally, as far as accomplishing whatever goal I'd set for myself when I was starting out. I'd go from $900 or $950 per month during the season to a $50,000 starting salary. I'd go from a $55 per diem to $125. There'd be health insurance, a pension plan, all sorts of benefits. Talk about a game changer! That kind of rags-to-riches bump would've changed our life-style, literally overnight.

That's why this cold shoulder from Dick Butler had me fuming, because there was so much riding on this one supervisor's take. It's like he held my future in the palm of his hand, and I didn't like it, not one bit. Felt kind of powerless against it. At the same time, I didn't know what to do about it. Kept me up nights, thinking it through. Wasn't anything to be done, really, but it was eating me up inside. Luckily, we were headed back to Portland after that series in Albuquerque, so I'd have a chance to sort things through with Kay and figure some kind of next move.

I actually called Kay that night from Albuquerque before heading home to Portland. Told her Dick Butler had come by and that I didn't think it went all that well. She knew what his visit could have meant for us. I said, "I don't know what it is, Kay, but that guy doesn't like me."

She said, "What did he say?"

I said, "Nothing, if you can believe it. Not a single thing. Asked me a couple questions and then just kind of walked away."

We talked for a while, and I mentioned that I was thinking seriously of quitting. As much as Kay hated the life and lifestyle of a minor league umpire, as much as she might have been on me to do something else, she didn't want to see me quit. Not like this. She said, "You really sure about this, Jim?"

I said, "No, I'm not sure at all. Just something I'm thinking about."

By the time she picked me up at the airport the next morning, my mind was made up. I was going to put together a letter of resignation, give my two weeks notice, and start looking for a new line of work. I was still young, still had that degree in education. There were any number of ways I could have gone.

I went out to the ballpark that night in Portland and told the guys on my crew what I was thinking. They tried to talk me out of it. They convinced me to sit on my decision for a couple days, until I had a chance to talk to Dick Nelson, our supervisor. It just so happened he was coming to one of our games that weekend and wanted to talk to us afterward, so we all figured something was up. Finally, a couple days later, I sat down with him and he filled me in. He'd heard I was thinking about quitting and he also asked me to sit on my letter for a bit. He said, "Jimmy, there's gonna be a change in the supervisory staff on the American League side."

I said, "What kind of change?"

He said, "I'm not supposed to say anything."

Then he told me what he wasn't supposed to tell me. Told me Dick Butler was going to be eased out to make room for Marty Springstead. Dick Butler would stay on in an administrative role, but Marty would be the eyes and ears on the field. He'd be the one doing the evaluating, here on in. This was huge, as far as us minor league hopefuls were concerned, because Marty was a veteran umpire. As far as I knew, Dick Butler had always been just a supervisor. I don't think he ever called a game in his life. The idea was that Marty Springstead would be more sympathetic, more appreciative, more open. There were no guarantees, of course, but Dick Nelson very strongly suggested I hold off on quitting for at least two weeks. This made sense to me. I mean, there were barely two full weeks left in the season, so what was it really costing me? And besides, there was a chance I could be picked to work the Coast League play-offs, and if that happened I'd be in line to earn some extra money.

Turned out to be the best no-decision I ever made, not handing in my resignation, because just a week or so later we were working a game at Cashman Field in Las Vegas when Marty Springstead came to town to check us out. It was a four-game series between the Vegas Stars, the Triple A affiliate of the San Diego Padres, and the Vancouver Canadiens, which at that time was the Triple A affiliate of the Milwaukee Brewers.

Marty actually came by and introduced himself before the first game of the series. Said he always hated how supervisors would sneak up on him when he was working, thought he'd try to do things a little differently. I remember thinking that was kind of cool, kind of decent. I'd always hated that surprise element, too. Felt like we were being ambushed instead of being evaluated as professionals, so I think we all appreciated his approach.

It was a four-game series, but after the third game Marty said he'd seen what he needed to see and that he had to move on to take in another batch of games in Portland. But then, after he left, we all got to talking, and I started to think Marty wasn't actually going anywhere. It didn't make any sense. First of all, it was well known among us umpires that Marty had a thing for Vegas, so why would he leave a day ahead of us when he could justify another night or two on the town? If you're a Vegas guy, you're a Vegas guy; you stay as long as you can. Plus, the series Marty'd said he was heading off to see didn't start for another night, so that didn't add up, either.

I said as much to my partners. I said, "Just be on your toes tomorrow, boys. Let's bust our asses and be sure to cover everything, because you never know."

Wouldn't you know it, Marty stayed in town for the last game of the series, only we didn't know it until it was over. Guess he didn't mind these types of surprises, after all, and it was a fortunate thing, too, because I ended up hustling on one particular play and it put me on his radar for good.

Here's the play: one out, runner on first. With a three-man crew, that meant the third base umpire had shifted toward second. I was on the line at first base, and the Vancouver batter hit a line shot to right field. At the crack of the bat, I took off in the direction of the ball, knowing it would be a catch/no-catch. That's what we call it when we hustle out on a fly ball—a catch/no-catch. Ninety-nine times out of a hundred, either the ball will drop cleanly for a hit or the fielder will make an obvious catch, but it's that one time that trips you up as an umpire, so you have to play it like it's that one time every time out. You have to hustle like you'll be making the call.

Well, I got about fifteen feet onto the outfield grass and the ball was sinking fast, and the right fielder dove and made one of those awesome, full-extension catches you see on the highlight reels. A classic catch/no-catch, and I threw my right arm up in the air and made the call on the run. Shouted it out, good and loud, for emphasis. But then I stopped, remembering the runner on first base and knowing the Las Vegas right fielder would now come up throwing to try to double him up.

Just then, I didn't think my partner in the middle of the infield would have time to make it all the way over to first to make the call, and the home plate umpire was also out of position, so I could see over my shoulder that it was my play to make. Somehow I managed to turn on my heel and start sprinting back toward my post at first, just as the right fielder sprang back up and started in on his little crow-hop to make the throw. I was busting my hump like you wouldn't believe, just to get back into position. Here again, most times the runner will be safe or out by a wide margin. He'll beat the play or he won't, but it'll be clear. But again, it's that one time in a hundred that you need to be in position, so that's all I could think about just then—to haul ass and put myself in the right spot for a close play at first.

Well, that Vegas right fielder bounced right back up after making his spectacular catch, unleashed a rifle shot back to his first baseman, and ended up nipping the runner by a couple inches. A real bang-bang whacker. And I was there to make the call. Punched him out with my fist, and with a loud yell you could hear all the way out in the bleachers.

I came off the field after that half inning feeling pretty good about myself. I'd busted my hump and put myself in position to make a tough call—*two* tough calls on the same play, actually. Doesn't usually happen that way, but that's how it went.

After the game, Marty Springstead came by the umpires' locker room. I took one look at him and said, "Aw, man. I'm glad to see you, Mr. Springstead."

And I was. I really and truly was. Because it meant that Marty Springstead had seen *me*. It meant he'd seen me hustle like crazy to make a call I probably wouldn't have to make. Twice. And it's not like I was in any kind of world-beater shape. It's not like another ump couldn't have done the same thing. But I was the one being evaluated, so it didn't much matter what any other umpire might have done. It only mattered what I had done and that Marty Springstead had been there to see it.

To this day, I tell that story to young umpires, reminding them to always work like there's a supervisor in town, to always hustle like it's that one play in a hundred. And to this day, Marty Springstead tells the same story from his end. He tells how he stayed on in Vegas for one extra game to catch the one play that would finally get Jim Joyce his shot at the bigs.

And it did. Marty ended up buying my contract at the end of the 1986 season and I was finally, mercifully . . . an American League umpire. Sort of. In reality, I was now just the property of the American League, but that put me one step closer to where I wanted to be.

The Call

ARMANDO GALARRAGA

I Can Only Smile

In Spanish, there is a saying: *Perdiendo se gana.* It means that for every bad thing that happens, there is a good thing that happens. In English, there is a similar saying: *Behind every cloud, there is a silver lining.* If you are fluent in Spanish and in English, you can see the sayings are very different, but when you translate they come out sounding almost the same.

Many people have said these things to me since the night of June 2, 2010, so first I must tell the bad thing that happens. First I must show the cloud.

I am one out away from a perfect game. It is very thrilling, very dramatic. Already there have been a lot of lucky things to get me to this place, a lot of lucky plays. But it is not only luck. I have thrown a lot of strikes. I have stayed ahead of the Cleveland hitters. There has been good movement on my fastball and a nice break on my slider. Probably it is the best game I have ever pitched, so I am happy about this. But I am not finished. There is still one more batter I must face: Jason Donald, the number nine hitter.

Jason Donald, the number twenty-seven hitter.

Jason Donald, the hungry hitter who almost beat me for a double in the third inning.

I repeat his name because it is the smallest name in the Cleveland lineup before the game, when I am going over my plan with my pitching coach. I do not say this to be disrespectful to Jason Donald. He is a starting player, yes, but he is in the very bottom spot of the batting order, so even his own manager does not expect him to be a dangerous hitter. He has been a major league baseball player for only one month, so he is here to get some experience, to show what he can do, to make his name bigger.

I decide before Jason Donald even comes to the plate that I do not like pitching to rookies in this type of situation. I have never been in this type of situation, but this is what I decide. Do not misunderstand: I am not afraid of Jason Donald. He does not intimidate me. I like the way I am pitching. My arm is strong. I feel like I can beat anybody with how I am pitching, even a Hall of Fame player. I do not think I have ever had more confidence as a pitcher than I have at this moment, but I do not trust this rookie. If I have a choice, I would like to pick someone else to be the last batter. I believe it is a bad recipe for me, to have to face someone with no history in the game, with all of his history in the future. He is out to beat me and I do not like that he is out to beat me.

The other Cleveland players, they have been out to beat me, too, but to Jason Donald I believe it means more. He is like

Trevor Crowe, the leadoff hitter, only I do not have to worry about Trevor Crowe for this perfect game. I am finished with him. He is in the on-deck circle, so if I face him again it will mean my perfect game is no more. It is only Jason Donald I have to worry about, and he is just a kid, the same way I am just a kid. He started the season in Triple A, just like me. He has something to prove, just like me. He knows the situation the same way I know the situation, the same way all the fans standing in Comerica Park know the situation. As much as I want Jason Donald to make the last out and give me a perfect game, this is how much he wants to get on base. His plan is the opposite of my plan. He does not want me to have this perfect game. He wants to spoil my perfect game, and I cannot blame him. It is his job to spoil my perfect game.

I start with a strike, looking. It is the story of my game, the first pitch for a strike. The home plate umpire, Marvin Hudson, he is giving me the outside corner all night, so I take it one more time. It is a good way to begin, I think. It is the only way to begin.

He is a good hitter, Jason Donald. A patient hitter. He is almost like a veteran player with his approach. He is one of those hitters who steps from the box between every pitch. He tightens his batting gloves, like Derek Jeter. He does a lot of different things to slow my delivery, to take me from my rhythm. This is very smart, I think. I did not notice this about him until now, because until now his at bats have not been so important. In the third inning and in the sixth inning, he came up with two outs and the bases empty so I did not watch him so carefully. Now there are also two outs and the

199

bases are also empty, but this at bat is very important. It is the most important at bat of the game. And so, yes, absolutely, I am watching him very carefully.

I think maybe I will try for this corner again, but then I think, *No, a slider, away.* It is a good pitch, but it is not a pitch for a strike. It is a pitch for an impatient, aggressive hitter to swing and miss, but Jason Donald does not swing, so it can only bounce in the dirt just behind home plate.

Now the count is 1–1. There is a lot of noise in Comerica Park. There is a lot of commotion. It is difficult to concentrate, but I am feeling good. My focus, I still have it. My confidence, I still have it. Jason Donald, he has it, too. He steps out again, and swings, and fixes his gloves. Then he steps back in. He is ready. He is matching his focus against my focus.

I go after my corner again, and this is what Jason Donald is expecting. He jumps on it. He hits a hard ground ball to the right side of the infield. I start running to first base as soon as the ball is hit. Miguel Cabrera starts moving to his right to make the play. He makes a nice play, actually. He is almost in the spot for the second baseman when he makes this play. Carlos Guillen, our second baseman, is already behind him and ready to field the ball. It is not an easy play, and as I am running I think once again that I am lucky to have Miguel on my team. Probably, if the ball goes through to Carlos, we will not have a chance, because Jason Donald is a fast runner.

From the side, I can see Jason Donald running hard to first base but this does not worry me. Already, we have made this play tonight, in the first inning. I like to make this play, a ground ball to the first baseman with the pitcher covering, so I am running very hard, very fast. I know I will make it to the base before Jason Donald, no problem. I do not have so far to run.

Miguel Cabrera makes a nice throw. It is a perfect throw, I think. It is a perfect play to end my perfect game. It is one last piece of good luck, which I can put together with all of the other pieces of good luck. I catch the ball and step on the base and I have time to think, *Yeah, all right, perfect game!* It is only a small second, but I am celebrating in my heart. I can see Miguel start to jump and celebrate. I can see Carlos start to jump and celebrate, too. I see all these things and feel all these things and think all these things, all in just one moment. My whole body wants to shout with happiness. I even start to throw my arms up into the air, but then in the very next moment, everything stops. Why? Because I hear the first base umpire Jim Joyce make the call for safe. I see his arms spread out to make the sign for safe. And I think, *No.* This is all I have time to think.

No.

After this, I must be honest, I do not remember too much. I have watched the tape of this play many times, so now I cannot say for certain what I remember from the moment and what I remember from the tape. The play at first base, I have watched it over and over. I can close my eyes and see this play. I can see it from the view of the camera, and I can see it from my own view. Baseball players, sometimes they say they can see a play in slow motion. A lot of athletes, they see things in this way. They have time to think about what is happening even while it is happening, and this is how I remember this play at first base. I remember running to first base and thinking, *Get me the ball, Miguel! Get me the ball!* I remember running so hard, so fast, I almost run past the throw, but then I reached back with my glove to make the catch. I remember making sure to meet the ball, to grab the ball, to squeeze it tight. I remember touching first base, and that it was not a gentle touch. I stepped very hard on the base, making very sure.

And then here is what I remember most of all. I remember that I smiled. It is what many people remember from this moment. All the time, people ask me how I can smile, at a moment like this, and I can only say that this is how my parents taught me. All the time, when I was growing up, they taught me that in hard moments I should always have a smile. It does not matter how you feel inside. It matters how you show on the outside.

This is why I cannot say anything to Jim Joyce after he makes his call. It is almost like I am the only person in the stadium who cannot say anything. I can hear Miguel Cabrera, he is yelling, "No!" He cannot believe it. I cannot believe it. The fans, they are yelling. My teammates in the dugout, they are yelling. Jim Leyland, he comes out to talk to Jim Joyce, and I cannot hear what he is saying but I think he must be yelling, too. Everyone is yelling, yelling, yelling, so there is no reason for me to yell. I do not have to say anything. I know the call should be out. Jim Joyce, I know he realizes the call should be out.

So I can only smile. I am too happy to do anything else. I know I have just pitched a perfect game. My whole body knows this. I am disappointed about this call. I am frustrated.

But I cannot be angry. I am too happy to be angry. I am so happy that even this call cannot ruin my happiness.

Miguel, he is fighting hard for me. He is riding Jim Joyce, yelling at him, calling him names. For a player to do this, it means a lot, because he will have to play in a game with Jim Joyce again. Tomorrow, he will have to play in a game with Jim Joyce again, but he does not care. He is a good friend, Miguel Cabrera. He is a good teammate. He does not care if Jim Joyce or the other umpires will be angry with him for being so angry at this call. He is telling the world what we all know inside.

Right now, all I want is for the game to be over. It goes on for a few minutes, all of this yelling. The fans are booing. Miguel, he cannot stop telling Jim Joyce how he missed the call, and I cannot find my focus. One moment, it is like looking through a tunnel, only at one thing, and now there is the noise and distraction from the whole stadium. Now it is like looking through a tunnel to the big, wide world.

The first thing I think, when the game starts again, is that I cannot pitch from a stretch. For the whole game, I have been pitching from a windup, and I worry that if I make a change I will lose my rhythm. Already I have lost my focus, so I want to make sure I do not lose anything else.

Jason Donald, he sees this. He is an aggressive player, a smart player. He sees that Miguel Cabrera is too busy yelling at Jim Joyce to pay attention to him, so he takes a big lead and runs to second base on my first pitch. Alex Avila cannot even make a throw, but it does not count as a stolen base. It is only because of indifference that Jason Donald goes to second, and it is a good name for this, *indifference,* because I do not care. It does not mean a thing to me. But then, two pitches later, Jason Donald does the same thing. I pitch from the windup again, and I do not think to hold him close, so he runs to third base. It is almost funny, the way he moves around the bases and nobody notices, nobody cares.

But then I realize what he is doing and I am worried. I do not want Jason Donald to score a run. Suddenly, this becomes very important to me. It is bad enough that I do not have my perfect game, but I do not want to lose my shutout at the same time, so I try to find my focus. There is another hungry rookie at the plate, Trevor Crowe, and he has worked it to a 2–2 count, and I do not want him to make good contact.

And here is my final piece of luck for this game: I do not make a good pitch to Trevor Crowe, but he only hits a high chopper to Brandon Inge at third base for the final out, and I can only think, *Okay, it is over.*

JIM JOYCE

Explosion

Talk to any athlete—any game, any level—and he'll tell you he wants the ball. A real athlete doesn't shrink from the play, or hide behind his teammates, or hope his number isn't called when the game's on the line.

Same goes for us umpires. We're working the same game, roaming the same field. We want to be in the mix. Doesn't matter if it's a blowout, or the top of the first in a meaningless game, or the last out of a no-hitter . . . we want in. Last out of a perfect game, same deal, and I'm hoping there's a play at first to decide this thing. That's how I was as a player, always wanting the ball hit to me, the game in my hands.

A lot of guys, they might not put it just this way, but I've never met an ump afraid to make a tough call. We're not cut that way. If we were, we wouldn't have gone into this line of work. If we were, we wouldn't have made it this far. But here it goes a couple shades beyond hope, that I'll get to make a key call to end this game. Deep down, I *know* the play is coming to me. And I *know* it'll be close. Yeah, we're taught to think this way, as umpires, but it goes beyond training, too. It's how we're wired. In fact, I'm so dead solid certain this thing will be decided down here at first base I can almost see it play out in my head before Galarraga goes into his windup. It's not that I'm psychic or anything, I'm not some whacko. It's just that it gets like that sometimes, out here on the field. You run through all these different scenarios in your head and you start to see things before they happen, but only because you've got every conceivable outcome playing out in your mind's eye. Whatever happens, whatever doesn't happen . . . you've already pictured it.

After more than thirty years, more than twenty of them in the bigs, there's nothing I haven't seen. Do the math. Thirty-something years. One hundred and fifty or so games a season. A couple hundred pitches per game. That comes out to about a million balls put in play, a million possible outcomes, and if it hasn't happened yet it's just not happening.

So that's where we are. Two outs, top of the ninth, and I know this next one is coming down to me. I've just got a feeling. Hunch, instinct . . . call it whatever you want. Can't say for sure if it's my training or my wiring, but here it is.

Jason Donald steps in for Cleveland and I tell myself to keep on my toes. I actually mumble these words to myself. Quietly, so no one else can hear, but I actually speak these words. Been on my toes the whole damn game, but now I'm on them most of all. Now I tell myself I need reminding. I look around the horn and see the other guys on the crew running through their own versions of the same thought. Marvin

Hudson, at home. Jim Wolf, at second. Derryl Cousins, our crew chief, over at third. In a flash, I imagine that what's running through their heads is pretty much what's running through mine. Can't imagine they're actually mumbling to themselves like I am—but hey, we've each got our own way.

Galarraga starts out Jason Donald the same way he's been starting out all these Cleveland hitters, all night long. Fastball, outside corner, for a strike. He's money, this kid, the way he's pitching. He can't miss. But Jason Donald is hanging in there, hanging tough. Got to hand it to him, he's not giving in. This late in the battle, it's all about posture, demeanor. It's how you move, and Jason Donald is moving like he's not backing down. Like he's got a plan. He's got this little routine going on, in and out of the batter's box between pitches, the way you see with a lot of hitters these days. He's got this icy stare, out at the pitcher. Some of these Cleveland batters, it's like they don't want to step in and face this kid but I don't get that from Jason Donald. He looks like he wants to do some damage.

Slider, low and away. Count evens at 1–1 and the crowd is going nuts, insane. Both benches are empty. It's one of those top-of-the-dugout-steps moments, everyone jostling for a good look. I've probably got the best damn view in the ballpark. There's Marvin Hudson behind the plate, and he's got more of what you'd call a front row seat, but he's so laser focused on the strike zone he can't take in the full measure of the moment. He can't see the pitcher, the batter, the catcher . . . the whole scene.

Jason Donald does his thing again. He steps out, adjusts, stares. His body language is exactly right, I have time to think.

He puts it out there that he's a tough out, and I'm guessing Galarraga is picking up on that. That always bugged me, back when I was pitching, when a batter was all antsy and fidgety at the plate. It can be a big distraction, and that seems to be this batter's game plan, to take Galarraga out of his rhythm, to shake him from his focus. To do whatever he can to get on base and get something going.

Jason Donald waits on the next pitch and lashes a hard grounder to the right side, looks for a beat like it'll get past Cabrera, the first baseman. The second baseman Guillen is right behind him, in backup position to make the play, but Jason Donald is busting it down the line and it looks like he'll beat the throw if the ball gets through. But it doesn't get through.

Cabrera fields it cleanly and turns back to the bag, and here's where the choreography of the game kicks in. Everyone on the field is in some kind of motion . . .

Pitcher does like he's supposed to and races to cover first.

First baseman does like he's supposed to and scoops the ball into his mitt and flips it back to his pitcher.

And I do like I'm supposed to and line myself up so the play is right in front of me.

All these moving parts, coming together at first base. Ball, batter, pitcher . . .

Umpires call it timing, when you get everything lined up in just the right way, and I have great timing on this play. Great positioning. Just like I've been taught. Just like I've been doing all these years, and just like I'd pictured it in my head, just before the pitch. I'm not saying this to blow smoke my own way, but it's all so right there, so perfect. Like it was drawn up in some Umpiring 101 course book.

At the time, down on the field, it feels like the kind of play we call a whacker. A bang-bang play, when the space between safe and out is a hair, a beat. A play like that, it just explodes in front of you—another one of our expressions. People ask me all the time, a play like that, how much of it is seeing, how much of it is hearing. I tell them it cuts about sixty-forty. You rely a little more on your eyes than your ears, but that doesn't mean you're not listening. No, you're listening hard for the smack of ball against glove, the thud of foot against base. So I tell people it's sixty-forty, but that's not really accurate. It is and it isn't—because, truth is, it's 100 percent of both. I know that makes the math a little screwy but there's no better way to put it. You're full on with your eyes, full on with your ears, and somewhere in there your gut checks in, too, so you're full on with your instincts. On a whacker, everything comes into play—so it's sixty-forty and 100 percent, all at once. Doesn't really make sense, I know, but when you've been umpiring as long as I have, that's how it all adds up.

At least, that's how it usually goes, but on this one bang-bang play I can't hear a thing. I don't notice it at first, that I'm not picking up the usual sounds of the game. It's only later, when I try to puzzle together what the hell happened. Don't know how or why or what went wrong. But in the moment, as the play's exploding, it's not even clear I need a sound track. I keep listening for it, and listening for it, but there's no thud of ball against glove. No footfall. No nothing. Don't think anything of it, at first. Like I said, don't think I even need my ears on this one. My eyes tell me the runner beat the throw. Plain and simple. No doubt in my mind. So I fling out my arms to show he's safe, and it's like a hush falls over the stadium. Place goes from completely nuts to completely quiet in the time it takes for me to make the call. Seventeen thousand people stunned into silence, just because I fling my arms wide and holler "Safe!"

Still, it takes a couple beats for me to get that somehow I haven't seen what they've just seen. Or, more likely, what they were hoping to see. Usually, we're all on the same page—most of us, anyway. Even when someone argues a call, half the folks will side with me, but here it starts to feel like I'm on my own. It starts to feel like there's me and then there's everybody else. The stunned silence turns into a rustling of boos and I start to get that these people are pissed. Soon as I make the call it comes clear. And it's not just the fans who don't like the call. It's the players, too. The coaches. Everybody. But it doesn't occur to me that I kicked the call. It's just not possible. I went against their expectations is all. This is what I tell myself, that I disappointed them. They'd already written the Hollywood ending to Armando Galarraga's performance in their heads, and now here I am shooting holes in the story. It's like I let the air out of the entire stadium—everybody kind of walks around deflated for a couple beats.

But then I catch a glimpse of Armando Galarraga and I go another way in my thinking. He's not jumping up and down, or yelling, or cursing. Just the opposite. He's smiling. That's it, just smiling. And it's not a wry smile or a mischievous smile or a mean-spirited smile or any type of smile with any kind of negative spin to it. It's just a regular smile. Then he turns back to the mound and our eyes lock for a split second, and in that split second his smile seems to get a little wider. It's almost like he's laughing.

I see that and I think, *Okay, Jimmy. Guess you got that sonofabitch right.*

The first indication anything is *really* wrong comes from Detroit manager Jim Leyland. Takes him all of five seconds to come out to talk to me, and it's not like he's in a hurry. Most times a manager comes out to argue a call, he comes running. Even when they're not moving so well, they're able to trot, but that's not the case here. Jim Leyland's in pretty good shape. He moves pretty well. But he's not moving now. He's just walking.

When he reaches, he asks what I saw. He's not all hot about it, like some managers. He's respectful. He's patient. Doesn't feel like he's trying to show me up or call me out. Feels instead like he just wants to make some noise for his pitcher, like he's out there to quiet the crowd.

I say, "Jim, he beat the play." Thinking this'll be the end of it.

He just looks at me, doesn't say anything.

So I repeat myself. I say, "What can I tell you, Jim? I've got him beating the play."

He still doesn't say anything. Just gives me a long, hard look. The whole exchange lasts only a couple seconds. Then he turns and walks back to the dugout so I step back to my post behind the bag and Miguel Cabrera starts giving me an earful. By this point, the guys in the dugout have ducked into the clubhouse and seen a replay on the monitors, and they're shouting out to their teammates on the field that Jason Donald was out. Saying it wasn't even close. At first Cabrera and the others aren't saying anything, but soon as word travels down the tunnel from the clubhouse and onto the field, he starts jawing at me. He's really letting me have it, and for the first time I start to think maybe I might have missed something. It's just a small sliver of doubt at first, because the fan and player reaction is a whole lot different than we tend to get on disputed calls. It's almost like it's personal. I try to tune it out but I can't. At first I hear it like folks are just plain disappointed, which I can certainly understand. But then the tone starts to change. With Cabrera, and with everyone else. I start to really hear it, and what I'm hearing is ugly, hateful, so I think it through. I realize there are monitors all over the stadium, at all the concession stands, and that tons of fans have their handheld devices that allow them to see instant replays, so even though they're not showing it on the big screen, hundreds of people have now had time to see this thing. In slow motion, probably. And that's when things start to turn. That's why.

All of this happens in no time at all—maybe a half minute, at most. Feels like an eternity, but that's just me, in the middle of it.

At some point during this half minute or so, I look over at Armando Galarraga, standing straight and tall over there on the mound. I'm still not ready to think I kicked the call. It's just a call at this point. I have no feelings of regret or sorrow. I have no feelings at all. Perfect game or no perfect game, it doesn't matter to me just then. It *can't* matter to me. I know that sounds cold, but that's umpiring. When you're calling a game, you don't care who wins or loses. You don't care about this or that milestone. All you can do is make the call, and then get yourself back into position to make the next one.

All you can do is all you can do.

The yelling and booing keep getting bigger, louder. The Tigers are so distracted they don't even bother to hold the runner. Jason Donald scampers around to third but nobody seems to care. Nobody seems to even notice, but somehow we all get through it. Somehow, they get the next batter to ground out to end the game and I'm thinking this'll finally be the end of it.

But then, soon as the game is over, everything kicks up a notch. The yelling. The booing. Even the small sliver of doubt I have out on the field, it starts to grow as I make for the clubhouse. It moves from the back of my mind to front and center, from a doubt to a worry, because I've never heard anything like this before. Folks are really letting me have it.

The rest of the crew, they've never heard anything like it, either. We leave the field together, and it's only later that I realize they're helping me to run a gauntlet. I'm the first one to say anything as we step into the tunnel on the way to the umpires' locker room. I turn to no one in particular and say, "Man, are they pissed!"

It's just a tossed-off comment, doesn't really mean anything, but as soon as I say it I want to take it back. Why? Because I say it in earshot of a couple grounds crew guys who happen to be in the tunnel. These guys work for the Tigers, so of course they're partial, and one of them thinks to respond. He says, "No shit!"

He says it in a kind of nasty stage whisper. It's meant for me to hear, but only a little, and it sets me off. Can't really blame the guy—I might have said a version of the same thing—but I can't really hear it, either. By now I'm a bit fried and frazzled so I let my emotions run away from me. I turn back to this grounds crew guy and make some feisty comment in response, and the two of us start yelling at each other. Very quickly it gets to where my guys have to step in and lead me away, push me toward the safety of the locker room, and as soon as we close the door behind us I turn to our crew chief Derryl Cousins and ask, "Did I kick it?"

He doesn't answer me right away, and this is when I know. Right in the middle of this one uncomfortable pause. It's just been a couple minutes, and I've gone from dead solid certain to a small sliver of doubt to now knowing full well that I cost this kid a perfect game, all on the back of Derryl not answering me straightaway. When you're right, your partner will let you know. He'll come right out and say it before you even have to ask. He'll say, "Don't listen to them, man. You were right on it." But here I have to ask, and for a beat or two he can't answer.

After another beat, he looks at me and says, "Jimmy, I'm so sorry, but from my angle I thought he was out. I'm just saying."

So now I know.

What happens next is all bunched together. Some of it I remember firsthand. Some of it I've had to puzzle back in place.

Long story short: I slip out of my uniform, down to my T-shirt, shorts, socks. Then I find a monitor and look at the replay. It's the one and only time I'll watch it and I can't believe what I'm seeing. The ball clearly beats the runner. All along, from the fan reaction, from the player reaction, I'm getting that I kicked it, but now I see it with my own eyes and I'm devastated. Right away I want to take it back, undo the damage. Right away it feels like one of the low, low moments of my life, and I don't see any end to it. I slump to a chair and drop my head into my hands. I say, "I can't believe I did this. I just can't believe I did this." Over and over, like a mantra. And really, I just can't believe it. It's like a bad dream, only worse, because with a dream you wake up and the bad stuff falls away. I'm shaking my head, beating myself up, trying not to fall apart. My partners don't know what to do with me. *For* me. For a while they just leave me alone to sit and think and smoke. You're not supposed to smoke in the locker room, but everybody looks the other way. I don't know what else to do with myself.

After a couple cigarettes I get it together enough to tell my partners to take off. I catch a look at the time, see it's barely nine o'clock. Normally it's ten o'clock when we get back to the locker room, maybe as late as eleven, but this game just flew. Normally we make a quick exit. My guys, they've showered and dressed, but they're hanging around, waiting on me. They're headed back to the hotel, out to dinner, wherever. Me, I'm headed out to Toledo to stay with my mom, but they don't want to leave me alone. They're not just my partners, these other umpires. They're my friends.

We've gone through a lot together. We'll go through a lot more—this, for one thing.

I hear someone tell Derryl Cousins the press is waiting. Apparently they've been waiting since we got here, but this is the first I know of it. The way it works, reporters can't enter our locker room unless we let them in. It's not like it is with the players, where the league and the players' union have it set up so the media have a certain level of access, guaranteed. Here, it's up to us. No guarantees. Doesn't usually come up, one way or another, but tonight it comes up. Tonight, we're the story—*I'm* the story.

They've been putting them off on my behalf, but now that I hear about it I want to wave them in. Figure I should just face it head on. Whatever it is, I should just face it. At first Derryl tells them to send in a pool reporter, thinking he or she can get the story and bring it back out to the group, thinks maybe I'll do a bit better one-to-one, but this starts a real pissing contest on the other side of the locker room door.

I can hear the whole thing from where I'm sitting.

"This is huge!" I hear.

"Come on, Derryl, just a few minutes."

"Let us in to talk to Jimmy."

Finally I just say, "Aw, what the hell. Let 'em in."

Derryl says, "All of 'em?"

I say, "All of 'em. Otherwise we'll never hear the end of it."

So Derryl opens the door and twenty, thirty reporters march into the locker room. No television cameras, just print and radio. Feels to me like they're about to descend on me, like a swarm, but that's not how it goes. Everyone is patient, civil, professional. There's a media relations guy from the Tigers, he's trying to help out, but it's still basically a scrum of respectful reporters, scrambling to get their questions answered. First one I hear is, "Have you seen the replay?"

I turn in the direction of the question and say, "Yep."

Next question: "So what do you think?"

I say, "I kicked the shit out of it, that's what I think."

Next question: "How do you feel about it?"

I say, "I feel like hell. This is a history call, and I kicked the shit out of it. And there's nobody who feels worse than I do. I take pride in this job, and I kicked the shit out of it. I feel like I took something away from that kid and I don't know how to give it back."

The rest is a bit of a blur because I break down at this point. Right then and there, I just start crying. Surprises the crap out of me, to be crying in front of all these reporters, but I can't control it. I have a vague memory of a guy in a red shirt coming over to pat me on the shoulder or maybe even give me a hug, tell me everything will be okay. To this day I've got no idea if it was a reporter or some guy from the Tigers organization or someone I already knew. This is followed by another vague memory of me putting my hands over my face and apologizing and excusing myself from all these reporters who were just trying to do their jobs. Don't know what pushes me over the edge but I suddenly feel like I can't be in the room with all these people, facing all these questions. Facing what I'd just done. So I slip into the back part of our locker room and try to gather my thoughts, my wits, whatever it is that needs gathering.

Most major league stadiums, the umpires' locker room is set up the same way it is here in Detroit. There's usually a main room about the size of a nice hotel room, where they've got a table set up with some food and drink, and maybe a couple couches or comfortable chairs. And then, off in the back, there'll be a smaller, more private room, which is just the locker room part. That's where I'm headed, to get away from all the craziness in the front room.

I'm just a mess. And my guys, they can see I'm a mess. One by one, they come back to talk to me. Or to sit with me. Marvin Hudson crosses to where I'm sitting and collects me in a giant hug. He says, "Jimmy, it's okay. It's gonna be okay."

And I say, "No, it's not." Underneath I'm thinking I didn't just screw the pitcher out of his perfect game, I screwed Marvin, too. He had the plate. It's a big deal for a major league umpire to work the plate for a perfect game. I cost him his own slice of history, and I say as much. I say, "I'm sorry, Marvin. This was your perfect game, too."

He says, "Don't worry about me, Jimmy. It's nothing."

Next guy to console me is Jim Schmakel, the clubhouse guy. He's from Toledo. I went to school with his brother, so we go way back. Soon as he sees me, leaned over a counter mumbling to myself about what's happened, he comes over to console me. He pats me on the back and says, "Don't worry, Jimmy. Everything's gonna be all right." Then, a couple beats later, he tells me he's taking me home, soon as I'm ready to head out.

Now, I've been working games in Detroit for years, so Jim Schmakel knows my routine, that I stay at my mom's house in Toledo, that it's all the way out of his way now that he lives up here in Detroit. And here he is, offering to drive me home, damn near two hours out of his way if you count the full round-trip.

I say, "I'll be fine, Jim. Thanks."

He says, "No, really. It's no problem. Let me take you home."

Couldn't have been nicer about it, but I can't see putting him out, so I thank him again and tell him I'll be okay. Then I look up and see the most unusual thing. There in the doorway is Jim Leyland, the Tigers manager. He's about the last person I'm expecting to see, here in the umpires' locker room. It pretty much never happens, that a manager comes by after the game. It's just not done. And yet here he is. He crosses over to me and sits down. He says, "Come on, kid. We're having a beer and a cigarette, put this thing to bed."

I say, "Jim, I appreciate it. I really do. I just can't talk right now."

So he puts his arm around me and says, "We don't have to talk. Where the hell are your cigarettes?"

I push my pack of Winston Lights across the table to him and he pulls out one for each of us. Then he reaches over to a bucket, where there are about a half dozen Miller Lites on ice. He grabs one for me and cracks it open, grabs one for himself and cracks it open. He takes a long swallow, then fires up his cigarette. Says, "You're not gonna join me?"

I take a long swallow to be polite, but soon as I do I feel like I might puke. I set the beer down on the table and reach for the cigarette instead.

"You know what?" Jim Leyland says. "You admitted to all those reporters you missed the call. Said you screwed up. I admire that."

All I can do is nod.

He continues: "But it's done. Nothing you can do about it, so let's just move on. The kid got a win. I got a win. Team got a win. End of the day, that's what counts."

Next guy to come into the locker room is Dave Dombrowski, the Tigers general manager. I look up and think, *Man, it's busy in here.* Can't remember a night when there was so much activity in our locker room. Usually it's just the four of us and the clubhouse guy. Tonight it's like it is after a play-off game, with so many people crammed into such a tight space. Someone else looks up and is clearly thinking the same thing. Says, "It's like a roomful of Jims in here." Meaning, there's me, Jim Leyland, Jim Schmakel, and Jim Wolf, my partner. Four Jims in all.

Dave Dombrowski comes by because he's a good guy and because he's heard my comments to the reporters, same way Jim Leyland must have heard, so now he wants to check on me, too. I hate that these good people are so worried about me, that I'm the focus of all this attention. He says, "Jimmy, you gonna be okay?"

I say, "Yeah, guess so. I'll be fine."

He tells me later that I didn't sound so convincing, but that's only because I'm not so convinced.

Here Jim Schmakel pipes in again. He says, "I'll take him home."

I say, "Jim, I already told you, I'm good. No need for you to ride me all the way back to Toledo. I can drive."

Then Dave Dombrowski tries to lighten the mood. He says, "Now you know what it's like to be general manager. Every day I hear about some trade I shouldn't have made, some trade I should've made. You can't win."

I try to smile, but I can't. I want to tell him it's not the same, but I can't. So once again, I just nod.

I'm smoking the entire time, lighting one cigarette with the butt of another. It's something to do to fill the time, something to distract me from what I've done. After a while, Jim Leyland stands to leave. He says, "Just so we're clear, it's over. We're good, right?"

I nod, to show that we're good. And I do appreciate that he's come by. I do.

Then Dave Dombrowski makes to leave. One more time, he says, "You sure you're gonna be okay, Jimmy?"

Truth is, I'm nowhere close to sure, but I say, "I'll be fine." Not a whole lot of conviction, but it's something to say.

He says, "Anything I can do, you let me know. Anything at all."

And just then it occurs to me. Something he can do. Something that might make everything as close to right as it can ever be. I say, "One thing, Dave. Can I talk to Galarraga?"

He's not sure he hears me right. "Now?" he asks, making sure. "You want me to set that up now?"

I say, "If you wouldn't mind."

Postgame

ARMANDO GALARRAGA

Big Belly

It takes a very long time for me to leave the field. I have to do an interview with the people from local television. I have to talk to ESPN, in English and in Spanish. There are many, many people who want to talk to me about this game. People in Venezuela want to talk to me, even. Already, I have heard someone call it the "almost perfect" game, and I do not like it, that it has only been a few minutes and there is already a name for what has happened.

Maybe later this will be okay, but right now I do not like it. It can be a perfect game or it cannot be a perfect game, but I tell myself it cannot be in the middle. It cannot be an *almost* perfect game.

The only person I want to see is my wife, Christin. I am looking for her and looking for her, but I cannot find her in the crowd. She always wears a bright orange T-shirt to the games when I am pitching, the color of the Detroit Tigers, so I can find her in the family section of the stadium, but it is not so easy on this night for me to find her. I am looking all over but I am also kept from looking by the reporters and my teammates and the other people from the Tigers. There is a lot of noise and activity. I am only wishing to be alone, but it is not possible for me to be alone.

The whole time, I do not have anything to eat. I do not have anything to drink, except when I first go to the club-house my teammates give me a beer shower. There is not a lot of beer to drink, only a few sips, but there is a lot of beer being sprayed and sprayed by my friends. It is a big celebration. They are congratulating me, like they do with champagne after a championship. They are trying to make it a special moment because they say it was a special game. They do not want the special moment to be ruined because it is not a perfect game.

But it cannot be ruined.

Before I talk to too many reporters, I talk to my father in Venezuela. It is important for me to have this telephone call because I know he is waiting to talk to me. He tells me every-body at home was watching my game and cheering for me. They put a special headline on ESPN, saying that Armando Galarraga is pitching a perfect game, and all of our friends and neighbors started watching. My whole family started watch-ing. My father says he is very proud of me. "I cannot believe it," he says. "My son has pitched a perfect game."

It makes my night to hear him say this. It makes me laugh, because of course I have not pitched a perfect game. I have, but only in a way, and so I have not. To my father, it is a perfect game. To my countrymen, too. This is what he tells me.

My mother, she also gets on the phone. She wants to tell me her feelings about the game. She wants to tell me that for the whole game, my grandmother was watching on the small television in her living room. She did not want to get up for the whole game because she did not want to make a change. She was all the way in Caracas and she thought the change would not be good for me, all the way in Detroit.

It makes my night to hear this, too.

And so I am talking, talking, talking in front of my locker. If I am not giving an interview, I am looking at my phone at so many texts and e-mails, or talking to someone from my family. I do not remember a time when I have been so connected to so many different people, when so many people have wanted to talk to me. I do not have time to even change from my uniform. My cleats, I am still wearing them. My pants, I am still wearing them. Only my jersey I have taken off, so I am only wearing my baseball shirt from underneath. It is like I am still dressed for work, for another game.

It feels to me like many hours have passed but it is only maybe a half hour, maybe an hour. It is not so very different from other games, when reporters want to talk to you if make an important play, but I am ready for the talking to finish. I am ready to find Christin and go home, because we have a new puppy and she needs to be walked. Also, because I am tired.

But I cannot go home yet because Dave Dombrowksi comes over to see me and tells me he would like me to go with him to the umpires' locker room to meet with Jim Joyce. I am very happy to do this. He is the general manager, Mr. Dombrowski. He is like my boss. But I do not go to meet with Jim Joyce because it is something I must do for my job. I go to hear what he has to say, because I want to meet him. I go because I have never heard of an umpire asking to meet with a player after a game. It is very unusual.

When I get to the locker room I see that most of the umpires are already showered and dressed. There is only me and Mr. Dombrowksi and the four umpires from the game. It looks like the umpires have already eaten. I can see their empty plates on the table. But Jim Joyce has not showered or dressed. I do not think he is eating. He is only sitting in the corner, by himself, looking very unhappy. When he sees me, he starts to cry. It is not a screaming cry, like for a child. It is a gentle cry, like for a man. He says, "My God." That is all. Just, "My God." Like he cannot believe it. Like he is heartbroken. Then he shakes his head back and forth and says, "I am so sorry, Armando. I do not know what else to say."

I do not know what to do about this, so I go to where Jim Joyce is sitting and I give him a hug. "It is all right," I say. "Mr. Joyce, this stuff, it just happens."

I am trying to say the right things, but I do not know the right things to say, so he does not agree with me. He says, "No, no, no. This stuff does not just happen. No."

I tell him, "Nobody's perfect." It is something I have already said to the reporters in front of my locker, to explain how a professional umpire can make a mistake on an important call. To say that we are all human.

So he tells me, "No, Armando. That's not true. Tonight, you were perfect. I feel like hell I screwed that up for you."

"It's okay," I say. "Do not feel bad for me."

"Of course I feel bad for you," he says. "I screwed up. You were perfect. Me, I was not perfect."

It is difficult for him to speak, I can see. Between his words, he is trying not to cry. He is very emotional. When we are finished with our hug he starts to walk around the room. Around and around. He is going back and forth like he cannot stand still, like he is very nervous. He is pacing, this is the word for what he is doing.

Dave Dombrowski becomes a little concerned, because Jim Joyce is a big man and he is so upset. I do not know, maybe Dave Dombrowski is worried Jim Joyce will have a heart attack, because he brings him a glass of water and tries to get him to take a drink. He tries to calm him down, but Jim Joyce cannot calm down so easily. He is too, too upset. His face, it starts to look like a red tomato.

The other umpires, they come to me to shake my hand. They can see their friend is very sad, very worried, so I think they are trying to change our meeting and make it feel more positive. They start telling me I pitched a good game, that they were proud to be on the field and be a part of such an important game. It is nice to hear the things they are saying.

After a while, I say good-bye to Mr. Joyce and the other umpires and when I get back to my locker I must talk to more reporters. Most of my teammates have gone home with their families. I am now the only Detroit Tiger player still in the clubhouse, I think, so I send a text to Christin to tell her I will take a quick shower and be ready in only a few more minutes.

The whole time, she has been waiting for me in the family waiting area, where it is very nice, very comfortable. I do not have to worry about her in there, waiting for me for so long, because she can be relaxed. At first she was hearing congratulations from the other families, from the wives of my teammates, but soon she is the only one left in the waiting area.

Finally I go to see her and she says, "What took you so long, Armando?" Like she is making a joke.

I laugh and tell her I have been a little bit busy.

She tells me she is very proud of me and I smile. Still, all this time after the game, I am smiling.

We go home to our new dog. Her name is Pansona. It is a Spanish name that means "big belly." She is an English bulldog. We got her the day before Valentine's Day but she is still a puppy. She cannot be left alone for too long. We go for a walk. Christin and I, we have a lot of energy, a lot of excitement from the game, so we do not wish to stay in the apartment. And the dog, she has been stuck in the apartment all night, so it will be good for her to be outside. We walk a few blocks from our apartment to a burger place we like called Sonic. We decide that we are hungry. It is late, probably around midnight, but we do not care. We have not eaten all night, we have been too distracted to eat, so we order cheeseburgers with fries and Cokes. It is like fast food, only better. There is a nice place to sit outside the restaurant, where the puppy can play in the grass and relax and eat. Pansona is hungry, too. Already we can see that this dog likes to eat. This is how she earns her name, because she is only a puppy and by now her belly is very big.

After our burgers, we walk back to our apartment, and we are surprised to see that our front door has been decorated with flowers and cards. We have only been gone a short while but there has been enough time for people to deliver these nice things, to show their appreciation. In the morning, we wake up to find a great many more nice things, like chocolate and stuffed animals and some nice bottles of wine.

It makes me feel very good that people I do not even know want to send me these presents. On the cards, they do not only write about the game, but also about everything that happened after the game. They write about how I could not be mad at Jim Joyce. How I am giving a good example for how to behave when things do not go the way you like.

At the stadium the next afternoon, I find out that there is a plan for me to meet Jim Joyce at home plate for a ceremony with the lineup cards. My manager Jim Leyland tells me about this before the game. It has all been arranged, if I will agree to it, so of course I agree to it.

In the middle of the ceremony there is a great surprise. My teammates, I can see them pointing and laughing and smiling. I am standing at home plate, shaking hands with Jim Joyce and posing for pictures, and I can see that my friends in the dugout are very excited. I look to where they are pointing and see a brand-new sports car, a red Corvette. It is not red like a cherry, but red like a wine, and there is someone from Chevrolet who is walking over to me to give me the keys. It is all part of the ceremony, like it has been arranged.

I cannot believe this. I am not expecting this, certainly. But it is a very nice surprise. The people from Chevrolet, they tell me after the ceremony that I can choose any Corvette I like, as a present from their company. The Corvette on the field is only for show. The one they will give me to keep, I will design for myself. I will pick the color, the interior, the extras. They will prepare it and present it to me later, in private, when it is ready. I am very excited about this because this is a favorite car of mine. But it is also a small trouble, because the Corvette I want to choose is a ZR1. It is a very special car, for racing. It is a car I have always liked. The car they are presenting to me for show, it costs about $60,000, which is a lot of money. However, the ZR1 will cost maybe $120,000, which is a lot more money.

They are both very nice cars. They are both more than I deserve. But I decide I do not care about such things. I tell the people from Chevrolet that I am so happy about their gift that I want to make a gift for myself. I tell them I want to pay the difference in the amount, so I can design the best car for me, and I am happy with this decision because it feels symbolic. It represents how I feel about the game against the Cleveland Indians. It shows how you can come so very close to something so very wonderful, so very special, and still not be able to reach it all the way. You can come close, but you cannot reach. However, it shows that you can sometimes reach the rest of the way if you give something extra, something of yourself.

At first I am a little embarrassed about this decision, because my belly is already so full. I am like my puppy with my big belly. People I do not even know are giving me presents and saying nice things, all because of this one special game, and it does not feel to me like I have earned all of these nice things. It feels to me like I can only keep trying and working hard so that soon I will be able to deserve them after all.

JIM JOYCE

Safe at Home

Next day, I've got the plate.

The whole night, it's like a carrot, the idea that I'll be right back out there on that same stage—center stage, this time. All eyes on me. I'm not too crazy about this last part, but it comes with the territory. It's not really the kind of job you can do in a vacuum, which I guess is what drew me to it in the first place. Anyway, it's the part about getting back out there and calling balls and strikes that keeps me going.

It's been barely twelve hours since I got back to my mom's house in Toledo, and in that time it feels like I've heard from the entire umpiring community. Calls, texts, e-mails. I've heard from my buddies, guys I used to work with in the minors, supervisors . . . up and down the line. And each one of them asks me if I'm okay to work this next game, if maybe I shouldn't just take a little time to decompress, let this giant uproar die down.

I appreciate the calls, each and every one, but it's not like I can step away from my job just because I screwed up. It's not like I'm some anonymous guy on the assembly line back at the Jeep plant and I can call in sick. It's tempting, believe me. I don't want to see anybody. More than anything, I don't want to have to face the Detroit fans. But at the same time, I know I have to head right back out there because if I walk away from this next game I'll just keep walking. I'll never get back to it.

I'm still not myself as I'm driving back out to the stadium. All I know is I need to get back to work, need to put that game behind me, but it's hard. The reason it's hard is because it's everywhere. Overnight it's become a big, big story. I try to avoid ESPN and the usual sports talk shows on the radio, but it's all over the place, what happened. It's on the front page of the *New York Times,* and even though I don't usually read the *New York Times* that kind of thing has a way of finding you.

You turn around and there it is.

One of the ripples that finds me this morning is the talk that baseball commissioner Bud Selig might consider overturning the call. This is something I've never even thought about but people are talking about it like it's a good possibility, so I start to think about it and I come away believing it's the absolute best thing that could happen. It's like a do over. A rewind button. I talk myself into it like it's a done deal—like I even have a say in the matter. I make the argument in my head: it's not like this one botched call had an impact on the rest of the game. The next guy was retired, so it wouldn't change the outcome. About the only stat they'd have to fix would be Jason Donald's batting average, trade his hit for an out, but it's not like he deserved the hit in the first place, so it'd be nothing for Bud Selig to wave his commissioner's wand and erase the whole mess from the record books.

Of course, I'm not thinking about baseball history or precedent or any of this stuff. I'm just thinking about me, and what I cost this kid pitcher, and how I can make it up to him.

So what do I do? I pull over on my way to the stadium and dial the commissioner's office on my cell phone. Figure I'll go straight to the top. I get the idea that if Bud Selig hears it from me that it's okay to switch the call, then maybe he'll do just that. I play out the whole conversation in my head.

Now, I've met Bud Selig over the years, and he's always struck me as a good guy, a decent guy, a real caretaker of the game, so I start telling myself he'll be my salvation. I have a whole argument worked out about the best interests of baseball, about sending the right message to our children, about doing the right thing.

But Bud Selig's not in, so I never get to make my pitch. Or maybe he's in and unavailable to take my call. Either way, I don't get to talk to him, but I leave word. I tell whoever is taking my message that it's Jim Joyce calling, and that it's okay with me if the commissioner calls me out on this, suspends me, whatever he has to do.

Here's the part where I catch myself wishing I still had to rub up a couple boxes of baseballs before the game. There's a lot going on at the stadium when I get there. A ton of interview requests. A huge pile of messages that have come in overnight. Soon as I get to our locker room I'm looking for a place to hide, and I start to think the peace and quiet of that old mud-rubbing ritual would be a good and welcome distraction right about now.

But that's not happening, so I sit at my locker with my head in my hands for what feels like the longest time. I try to tune everything out and focus on the game. When you work the plate, there's a certain amount of preparation you need to do. Not a lot, but some. It's different than working the bases. You need to know who's pitching, his tendencies, his history. You need to study the lineups, maybe get a feel for who's playing well, who's slumping, that sort of thing. You want to gather as much information as you can, so you have some idea what to expect. A lot of guys, they've been doing this long enough that they can sometimes just wing it, but I've never been one of those guys, so I do what I can to get my head around the game.

Turns out it's not so easy, today of all days. Turns out there's a whole media circus set up at Comerica Park, coming off last night's game. I'm not too crazy about any of this, but I don't want to go against it. They've set it up so Armando is getting a new car from a local dealer and I don't want to be the guy who keeps him from getting a new car. I've already cost this kid enough, so I tell the media relations guys I'll go along with whatever Armando wants to do. If he's on board, I'll be on board. If he's uncomfortable or if it gets to be too much, then that's okay, too.

There's a whole ceremony at home plate, me and Armando exchanging lineup cards, shaking hands, making a public show of apology and forgiveness. The folks in charge have made it into a real nice moment. I don't mind it, but I wish it would all go away. I wish the game could just start so I can lose myself behind the plate. I get to thinking it's like a real-life game of tag, like we used to play as kids. Remember? If you were on base, you were safe, protected. If you were running around, you were a target. That's how I start to look at this next game, the day after I kicked the call. It feels to me like the whole world is pulling at me, tugging on me, pushing me in this or that direction like there's this big red bull's-eye on my back and the only way I can make it stop and find any peace is to put on my umpire's mask and stand behind home plate and get back to work. It's the only place I'll feel safe. *Home*. Just like we used to call it when we were playing tag.

I'm crying as I shake Armando's hand at home plate. I'm wiping away the tears by pinching at the bridge of my nose, like I've got a headache.

I'm thinking, *Let's just play ball already.*

Soon we do just that, but the noise surrounding this game doesn't go away. For a long time, it doesn't go away. I start to hear from people all over the country . . . all over the world, even. Seems we've struck some kind of chord, me and Armando. Me, for the way I copped to my mistake and apologized and took my lumps. Armando, for so graciously accepting my apology and for carrying his disappointment with such dignity and good cheer.

Wasn't how either one of us wanted to see this thing play out, but here it is, and over the next days and weeks I'm bombarded with the thoughts and good wishes of tons of well-meaning folks from all walks of life. Two of these exchanges stand out in particular. The first one finds me at an airport security gate as we're leaving Detroit that evening. I'm about to go through the X-ray machine and I catch this one security officer standing off to the side, staring at me like he knows who I am. He's got a drug-sniffing dog at his heels, so he's clearly on the job, but he keeps checking me out. Finally, as I pass through the metal detector, he approaches and says, "I just want to thank you, man."

I'm not sure I hear him right, so I flash him a confused look. Really, I've got no idea what this guy is talking about. I say, "Thank me? I'm the one who should be thanking you. You're the one on the job. You're the one keeping us safe."

But he just shakes his head and points at me and says, "No, thank *you*."

And then I finally put two and two together and realize he's talking about the game. From here on in, it'll start to feel like this is all anyone wants to talk to me about, but this is the first I'm realizing it. My face is plastered around the terminal. Every screen in every bar is tuned to ESPN or CNN, and everywhere I look I see my face.

The second exchange is even more meaningful, more uplifting. I get an e-mail the day after the game from an eleven-year-old kid named Nick Hamel, who is suffering from spina bifida. The e-mail comes to me through Phil Cuzzi, a fellow major league umpire. It shows up in my inbox later that night and my wife Kay takes a look at it before I do. She's blown away by what she reads, so she calls me first chance she gets and reads the e-mail to me over the phone.

> Please tell Mr. Joyce to hang in there, keep his head up, and give him a hug for me the next time you see him. My physical therapist once told me, when I got upset over not

being able to attend baseball games for four months due
to complications from brain surgery, not to fret over spilled
milk. At first I didn't understand but eventually i [sic] figured
it out. She was telling me yeah it stinks but things could
have been worse, in the grand scheme, it was just spilt
[sic] milk.

I know Mr. Joyce doesn't feel that way now, as i didn't then,
but eventually things will settle down and it will fall into the
spilt milk category. You guys have a tough job and you all
do it well . . . better than anybody else that is why you are in
the big leagues.

Take care,

Umps [sic] best friend, nick.

It knocks me to the floor, what this kid wrote, and then
when Kay tells me he's just eleven it knocks me down all over
again. To think that this kid would take the time to look up
from his troubles and reach out to me . . . it's just astonish-
ing. And so, soon as I can get to a computer, I shoot this kid
a return e-mail and we start corresponding. Right away, I get
that this is one special kid. His e-mails just about break my
heart. He writes about how he's a huge baseball fan but says
he doesn't really have a favorite player. Mostly he just follows
us umpires. He knows about our careers, our paths to the
bigs, all of that.

You have to realize, I've been doing this a long time, but
I've never come across an umpire nut like Nick before. Truth
is, I don't know what to make of all this at first, but then I

think about it and it starts to make sense. I mean, spina bifida is a pretty debilitating birth defect. It's horrible, really. This poor kid is in a wheelchair, can't really move around, can't really talk without a great deal of effort, so of course he's not about to see himself out there on the field, chasing down fly balls or stealing bases. But umpiring? Calling balls and strikes and enforcing the rules of the game? That he can maybe see himself doing, wheelchair or no, so he falls in to following us.

Anyway, that's how his dad explains it to me, because once Nick and I start corresponding I start hearing from his dad, too. We're sending e-mails back and forth. Nick keeps seeing all the crap I'm getting in the media, people saying nasty things about me costing Armando his perfect game, and he keeps taking it on himself to pick me up. The kid's eleven years old, confined to a wheelchair, needs a ventilator to help him breathe . . . and *he's* telling *me* to hang in there. He's telling me to be strong. Pretty incredible stuff. Like something is really, really wrong with this picture. Like it should be the other way around.

Turns out there's a game on my schedule not too far from where he lives, so I arrange for tickets for Nick and his family and they all come out to the ballpark. Let me tell you, I'm more excited to meet this kid than I've ever been to meet anybody in all my years in baseball. We arrange to meet a couple hours before the game so Nick and his family can take in batting practice and get the full ballpark experience.

And get this: the kid shows up at the stadium in an umpire's cap. It fills my heart when I see this cap on his head. It's a pretty ratty cap, though. Looks like Nick has been wearing it a long, long time. It occurs to me he should probably have a new one, so I say, "Listen, Nick. You need an official umpire's hat." I take the cap off my head and put it on his. I do this without thinking about it. Same hat I was wearing that night in Detroit.

His face lights up like it's his birthday ten times over. He doesn't know what to say, but I'm not finished. There are some things I need to tell him about this hat. I say, "This is a special hat. This is the hat I was wearing that night I kicked the call. Nobody's asked me for it, but they might. The people at the Hall of Fame, they've got Armando's shoes and his uniform. They've got the first base bag. So if someone from Coopers-town calls and wants this hat, I'm gonna have to come back and get it from you."

Just in case anyone's wondering, I'm hoping the Hall of Fame never calls.

Couple weeks later, it gets to where I can joke about it, and it's because of big-hearted people like Nick that I'm able to keep what's happened in perspective. I'm working a game in Cleveland, at first base. Indians versus Royals. Jason Donald gets on base and I decide to mess with him. First time I've seen him since the Galarraga game. The Kansas City pitching coach goes out to the mound, so I sidle up to Jason Donald during the break and say, "You know what, kid? I should really be pissed at you."

Surprises the crap out of him, that I'm even talking to him. At a time like this. Me, of all people.

He turns to me—stunned, intimidated, confused—and says in his most respectful voice, "Why is that, Mr. Joyce?"

I'm busting up laughing inside, because this rookie's got no idea where I'm going with this. But I try to play it straight. I keep to my stern, umpirelike demeanor. I say, "Because you did your job that night in Detroit, young man. You busted your ass down the first-base line. Most guys, they'd just take their time on a play like that. But not you. You had to go run that thing out like a scared hare."

He can't tell if I'm being serious, doesn't seem to know what's expected of him. I've put him in a tough spot. He says, "Mr. Joyce, I meant no disrespect to you at all."

Now it's me who doesn't know what to make of this whole scene. Now we're moving in a whole other direction. I say, "What are you talking about?"

He says, "That night, after running through the base. The way I responded. I'm really sorry."

I have no idea what he's talking about, so I soften and say, "Jason, I'm just busting your chops. What the hell are you talking about?"

He starts to explain, apologize, whatever, but then the pitching coach leaves the mound and we have to get back to the game. I keep thinking the kid'll get back down to first base and we can finish the conversation but it never happens, so after the game I ask the clubhouse guy if he's got any idea what Jason Donald meant. Together, we figure he must have thrown up his hands, or celebrated, or responded to the call in some way he now regrets, like he couldn't believe I'd just called him safe.

But I never saw any of that. I'm just busting his chops for busting his ass—because, really, if Jason Donald hadn't been so damn hungry, I wouldn't be in this mess, now would I?

Appendix

BOX SCORE

Wednesday, June 2, 2010
Comerica Park, Detroit, Michigan

```
              1 2 3 4 5 6 7 8 9    R H E
Cleveland  0 0 0 0 0 0 0 0 0 — 0 1 1
Detroit    0 1 0 0 0 0 0 2 X — 3 9 0
```

Cleveland	AB	R	H	BI
T Crowe cf	4	0	0	0
S Choo rf	3	0	0	0
A Kearns lf	3	0	0	0
T Hafner dh	3	0	0	0
J Peralta 3b	3	0	0	0
R Branyan 1b	3	0	0	0
M Grudzielanek 2b	3	0	0	0
M Redmond c	3	0	0	0
J Donald ss	3	0	1	0
Totals	28	0	1	0

Detroit	AB	R	H	BI
A Jackson cf	4	1	3	0
J Damon lf	4	1	1	0
D Kelly lf	0	0	0	0
M Ordonez rf	4	0	1	1
M Cabrera 1b	4	1	2	1
B Boesch dh	3	0	1	0
C Guillen 2b	3	0	0	0
B Inge 3b	3	0	0	0
A Avila c	3	0	1	0
R Santiago ss	3	0	0	0
Totals	31	3	9	2

E S Choo (3, throw).
DP Detroit 1, Cleveland 2.
HR Detroit M Cabrera (15, 2nd inning off
   F Carmona, 0 on, 0 out).
RBI M Ordonez (35), M Cabrera (49).
SB A Jackson (8, 2nd base off F Carmona/M Redmond).

Pitchers Cleveland	IP	H	R	ER	BB	SO
F Carmona (L, 4-4)	8.0	9	3	2	0	3

Detroit	IP	H	R	ER	BB	SO
A Galarraga (W, 2-1)	9.0	1	0	0	0	3

U—Marvin Hudson, Jim Joyce, Jim Wolf, Derryl Cousins
T—1:44. A - 17,738.

Acknowledgments

I would like to thank my family, my friends, and my teammates for helping me to become the person I am today. Also, I would like to thank the Detroit Tigers and the Detroit fans, for treating me with such kindness, as well as my agents—Jeff Feinstein, Cesar Sanchez, Fernando Cuza, and all of the nice people at SFX Baseball—for taking such good care of me and my career. Also, I would like to thank Barry Terry of The Landmark Forum, for his special guidance! And finally, I want to thank Dan Paisner, Mel Berger, and Jamison Stoltz, for helping me to tell my story.

A.G.

This is a list of just some of the people who have in one way or another played a significant role in the development of this part of my life and my family's life. I thank each and every one of you for your support, and for the parts that you have played in this story. From the bottom of my heart . . . thank you: Dan Paisner; Mel Berger; the good people at Grove/Atlantic; Derryl, Marvin, and Wolfie; the Detroit Tiger fans, and the fans across the country; Jim Leyland; Dave Dombrowski; Jim Schmankel; the entire Detroit Tiger organization; Bud Selig; Major League Baseball; Cathy Davis; Don Denkinger and Larry Barnett; Mike Port; Mike Teevan; George Hanna and Bob Campbell.

JJ.

A grateful tip of the pen to my friend and agent Mel Berger, of William Morris Endeavor, and his assistant Graham Jaenicke, for helping to get this project off the ground; to Jamison Stoltz, Morgan Entrekin, and the rest of the Grove/Atlantic team, for sparking to this story; and, mostly, to Armando Galarrage and Jim Joyce, for allowing me into their lives and for shining a light on the enduring importance of humility, forgiveness, and abundant good cheer.

D.P.